HELLO CHAMPION

GOD WANTS YOU TO Win!

We invite you to put your foot in the stirrup,
swing up into the saddle, and "enjoy the ride".

Come visit our website
www.jeffcopenhaver.com
(Many of these stories are there on video.)

God Wants You To Win

© 2017 Jeff Copenhaver

Printed in the United States of America

Design and Layout by Ken Fraser • www.ImpactBookDesigns.com grafxedge@gmail.com   **Cover and photoshop by Cody Stromberg**

Jeff Copenhaver Ministries
P.O. Box 37
Rainbow, TX 76077
www.U2win.org   www.jeffcopenhaver.com

Introduction

As a young boy growing up in rodeo, my boyhood dream was to be a world champion just like my father. Little did I know that there was much more to becoming a champion than my six year old's perspective.

Years later after I had received Jesus as my Lord and Savior, He spoke in my heart that a champion is someone who changes their world everyday – for the good – with the love of God! If you are a born-again Christian, you have the King of Kings, Lord of Lords, and Champion of Champions living in you. His heart becomes your heart – the heart of a champion.

In the third chapter of Phillipians, the apostle Paul says that he counts everything in life worthless when compared to one thing – knowing Jesus Christ. His whole life purpose was to know his savior intimately and to understand and fulfill the purpose that Jesus had for his life.

I believe that God is raising up people in every walk of life all over the world. The business, political, sports, agricultural, educational, entertainment, musical, medical, and yes, the rodeo world. Men and women full of the Spirit of God, the Word of God, and the love of God; empowered to change their world.

Jeff and Deb

May this devotional help direct you to the One who loves you more than you can ever imagine and encourage you to become a champion for God! Growing up, I wish someone could have freed my thinking with this good news – God wants me to win in every area of my life and truly my friend:

GOD WANTS YOU TO WIN!

"In a race, everyone runs but only one person gets the prize. So, run your race to win. To win the contest you must deny yourselves many things that would keep you from doing your best. An athlete goes to all this trouble just to win a blue ribbon or a silver cup, but we do it for a heavenly reward that never disappears…." (1Cor. 9:24-26, the Living Bible)

Jeff and Sherry Copenhaver

Jeff is the 1975 World's Champion Calf Roper, the son of two-time World Champion Bronc Rider, Deb Copenhaver- father and son World Champions. In 1986 Jeff and Sherry started America's *first* Cowboy Church at Billy Bob's in the historic Ft.Worth, Texas Stockyards. Jeff and Sherry now travel nationally and inter-nationally teaching roping schools and motivating others to be champions for the Lord!

"We hope that **God Wants You To Win!** inspires and stirs up the champion in you! We are available to speak at your church, school, or organization. Jeff continues to train breakaway and tie-down calf ropers." **contact us at jeffcopenhaver@gmail.com**

YOU ARE A CHAMPION!

If Christ be in you, you are a champion.

If your heart of hearts has received the King of Kings, then you are a champion.

You are a champion, even if you are down and out.

You are a champion, if it's hard right now to shout.

You are a champion, if you're standing tall on the podium.

You are a champion, if disappointment has made you numb.

You are a champion, if the times are rough right now.

You are a champion, if on your knees you'll bow.

You are a champion, not made to bow to sin.

You are a champion, from your very core within.

You are a champion, with gifts and talents to spare.

You are a champion, not bowing down to cares.

You are a champion, no longer holding back.

You are a champion, not bound by fear and lack.

You are a champion.

Think like a champion.

Speak like a champion.

Act like a champion.

Love like a champion.

Compete like a champion.

Live like a champion.

GO FOR IT!

1Cor.15:57

"Arise (from the depression and prostration in which the circumstances have kept you - rise to a new life)!
Shine (be radiant with the glory of the Lord), for your light has come, and the glory of the Lord has risen upon you!"
Isaiah 60:1

Table of Contents

Snoopy

---◦◦◦◦---

*I*t was June of 1975 and I was almost half way through the year on the quest for a calf roping world championship. I had flown from somewhere in California to Phoenix. My truck and trailer and horse were there, so I was driving again. I was on my way to rodeos in Cortez, Colorado, and Pleasant Grove, Utah.

Well, my truck broke down at Williams, Arizona; now I have to charter a plane. I made it to Cortez and placed with a 9.3 second run - but no good at Pleasant Grove. From Pleasant Grove three of us chartered the same pilot to get to the slack the next morning at Roseburg, Oregon. As we're flying across Utah and Nevada, our pilot goes sound asleep with the plane on automatic pilot. We were all asleep except Mike Ring, my bulldogger friend. He woke up as we are heading directly into the only mountain in that whole area. That was the first bullet I ducked. We got to Roseburg, where I roped two calves that morning in the slack. My next mission was to get to Portland International Airport pronto to catch a commercial flight to Edmonton, Alberta to compete the next day at St. Albert, Alberta, Canada. I was the only one left in the plane with the charter pilot. Away we go!

A few minutes into our flight our engine started to sputter, we're running out of gas on one tank. The pilot said: "don't be alarmed, I'm switching over to the other tank." Well, I'm not a rocket scientist, but I did notice that the needle on the gauge of the second tank hardly moved. Sure enough, a few minutes later the engine is sputtering! "Houston – no - Jeff, you have a problem!" My pilot began to lose all the color in his face. We began to circle and lose altitude as we looked for a possible place to land. Would you believe we see a semi-deserted, half-baked runway with an old crop duster plane parked there? By the grace of God we landed. I jumped out of the plane and ran to a little tin shed where a crop duster pilot was sitting on a chair with his feet propped up. He was sound asleep. I came running and hollering. "Can you fly me to Portland International? I've got to get there immediately!"

He didn't reply, he just started running to the plane. He pointed to the second seat of an old Snoopy plane and said, "Get in the back – buckle up!" I wedged my rope can (my only luggage) in front of me and was buckling up as the plane began to move. He wasted no time on normal take off procedures. He took off and banked the plane about four feet over some trees –we were gassing it to Portland. He dropped me off and told me which way to go to get to the terminal where my flight was soon departing. I ran and ran and ran some more and finally got to my gate. At that point, a young lady informed me that I was too late. Wrong! I said, "That can't be - this is a maximum emergency. I have to get on this plane." She went down the aisle way to the plane with me. We actually knocked on the outside of the plane door to let me in. I know, this sounds crazy! It was! But, guess what – they opened it!!! I got on the flight in a full sweat!

Off to Edmonton – I got there and rented a car to St. Albert which is just outside of Edmonton. This time I was actually there a few hours ahead of time so I could look around and see whose horse I could borrow. In rodeo, when you use someone else's horse, you pay them 25 per cent of your winnings. Well, the only horse that I really knew was a bay horse owned by Roy Mc Peak. This was a real nice horse except for one major obstacle – he was so quick in his stop that if you didn't do things close to perfect, he would rocket you into the ground like a spike in a log. In spite of this I decided to ride him.

As you look at this roping picture you can see me getting off old bay. This has to be the weirdest twinkle-toe ballet roping picture I've ever seen – that's because I was so close to being violently thrown to the ground. Good news, I won St. Albert! This whole story was Thursday to Sunday in June of 1975. Placing at Cortez and winning St. Albert moved me into first place for the first time that year - and I was still alive! Hey, Champion – is it going to be easy? Could it get scary? Will you need to be creative? Will exhaustion set in? When you pursue your dream, you're in a battle. Overcoming obstacles becomes your stairway to victory!

Go For It!!

II Chron. 15:7, *(God's Word Translation)*, *"But you must remain strong and not become discouraged. Your actions will be rewarded."*

Jeff at St. Albert, Alberta 1975

Just One More

s a boy I can remember having such a desire to become a top calf roper. One of the common syndromes for serious ropers was the inability to be able to quit a practice session. The common phrase was "Just one more."Now, there is a major flaw in the "Just one more" theory, and a *theory* was all it ever was. It definitely wasn't reality. Here's why one more calf to rope and tie. or one more run down the rope wasn't enough. If you were having a great practice session, you definitely didn't want to quit. If you were having a bad session you couldn't quit because you can't quit until you get everything ironed out.

Nevertheless, no one - myself included - ever said "Well, let's tie about 50 more and we'll hang it up for the day." Nope, that didn't happen. It was always - in all fraudulent sincerity —"just one more." I believe another reason I kept saying "just one more" is that I was doing what I loved to do – roping and tying calves as fast as I could go, and loving every minute of it.

Let me ask you something. What is it that you love to do so much that you hate to quit? Is it just one more hour practicing the guitar? Just one more recipe out of *Southern Living*, or just one more business deal successfully negotiated? When we give our lives to Jesus Christ He loves to reveal to us the desires, the gifts, the talents and abilities He has placed in us. He wants these desires *fulfilled*, not frustrated.

Eric Liddell, the Olympic Gold Medal winner in the movie *Chariots of Fire* (a true story), made the statement "I feel my Father's pleasure when I run." To him, the "just one more"was one more stride or one more race. Liddell used the platform of being a world class athlete to share his love and faith in Jesus Christ. Maybe you're not sure what passionate desire God has placed in you. If not, ask Him, Yes, it's just that simple - just ask HIM.

The Holy Spirit will begin to reveal to you the thing you enjoy to do so much that you begin to say "just one more". For instance, Johnny, come and eat –"Ok, Mom, but I've got to make "just one more basket." People who have a burning desire to develop their God-given gift need "just one more!" Is this article over? No, I've got to write –just one more sentence!

Go For It!

Phil. 3:12, *(God's Word Translation), "It is not that I've already reached the goal or have already completed the course, but I run to win that which Jesus Christ has already won for me.*

**Jeff Copenhaver at Edmonton
Alberta, Canada 1989**

Champions Know God Is Never The Problem

t was the early 1980's and I was excited to be competing at the San Antonio rodeo. As a young Christian, I had prayed and told God that I sure needed to win something. (C'mon, you've done the same thing.) Well, I didn't win - big disappointment. If I'd admitted it, I was a little bit griped at God.

Suddenly the Holy Spirit spoke loudly in my spirit and said, **"I'm not the problem!"** What a shock! Little did I know what these four words would do for my outlook, my attitude, my life and my walk with God. **Hebrews 13:5** says, *"I will never leave you nor forsake you."*

No wonder the Lord spoke so loudly in my heart that morning when He said *"I'm not the problem."* <u>He is not your problem.</u> In fact, <u>He's always the answer</u> to every problem or life's questions. But you ask, "If God is not the problem, then what is?" Why all the killing and destruction and tragedy in the world? I'm so glad you asked that. **John 10:10** says, *"The thief (or satan) comes not but for to steal, to kill and destroy."*

When I was a boy there was a movie called "The Invisible Man." It was about this guy who (because of a scientific experiment) became invisible. He could hide in a room full of people; he could punch someone and they couldn't see where it was coming from. Here is your picture of an invisible enemy (a spiritual enemy). **Eph. 6:12** (nlt), *"For we are not fighting against flesh-and-blood enemies, but against evil rulers and authorities..."*

Yes champions, we have an unseen enemy, and he is the master of evil. But the good news is that he has been defeated. I John 3:8 reads, ". . .for this purpose the Son of God was manifested, that He might destroy the works of the devil." How many people have you been around who are mad at God because they lost a loved one, their child went to prison, they had a financial disaster or something else that convinced them to buy a lie? You think God's your problem-He let you down! He didn't come through for you. Read **Hosea 4:6**, *"My people are destroyed for lack of knowledge."* **James 4:7**, *"Therefore submit to God, resist the devil and he will flee from you."*

Here is another key, first we submit to God, then we must resist the devil – tell him "in Jesus' name" to leave every aspect of your life! (speak the scripture out loud that pertains to your situation) Since that moment the Lord spoke in my heart *"I'm not the problem,"* I've never even been tempted to be mad at God again! When I'm going through a difficulty of some kind, or feel like the captain at the helm of the *"Perfect Storm,"* I know God is on my side. He's my loving Father, my best friend, the One who really loves me

Champions know God is NEVER the problem!

Go For It!

I Peter 5:8, *"Be sober; be vigilant; because your adversary the devil walks about like a roaring lion, seeking who he may devour."*

Romans 8:31 (NET), *What then shall we say about these things? If God is for us, who can be against us?*

Jeff at the NFR in Oklahoma City 1974

Jeff 12 years old, Buddy 12 years old, Lee Richmond 10 years old,
Winning our trophies at Coeur'd Alene, Idaho

Buddy

⚬⚬⚬⚬

*I*was 12 years old in 1961 and about the happiest boy in the whole world. We lived in Post Falls, Idaho and my dad brought me a special present all the way from Texas. It was a calf roping horse and his name was Buddy. He was trained by and named after Buddy Groff, a runner up world champion calf roper. Immediately we became "best buddies." He was just what I needed at my age. He was gentle, yet he had some speed. Buddy was the perfect "first good horse" a boy could hope for. Years later, I would ride my horse Streak to win a world's championship; but I believe Buddy was the most important horse in my roping dreams. I loved Buddy beyond description!

My folks were going through a hard time in their marriage. Two years later it led to divorce. Consequently, getting out of the house and going for a ride on Buddy was as good as it got! Check out this picture of Buddy. He was about 14'2" hands, weighed about a thousand pounds and had a kind eye. He was perfect; he was "My Buddy."

He was the first big step in the pursuit of my dream to be a champion! **Proverbs 18:24** says, *"A friend sticks closer to you than a brother."* For over 30 years now I've known the best "Eternal Friend" that anyone could ever know! Jesus Christ! I was introduced to Him as a young boy around 12 years old. My family didn't know God but they wanted my sister and me to go to a little church in the mountains; it was there that we first experienced the joy and love of Jesus!

Years later after winning a world's championship I realized that I hadn't pursued my relationship with Him. Life (even at the top) had no purpose or satisfaction for me.

I began to search for that closeness with my "eternal friend". My time with Him felt like saddling up and riding Buddy!

The previous picture is me winning the calf roping at a junior rodeo in Coeur d'Alene, Idaho on Buddy. Standing next to me is my special friend Lee Richmond. This couldn't have been better for me than if I had just won Cheyenne.

Question:...Have you ever come to know your "best Buddy?" He loves you so much! I'm talking about the very one that created you, died for you and then prepared for you an "Eternal home in Heaven." JESUS! Everybody needs a Buddy!

God Wants You To Win!

John 15:15 *(nkjv), "No longer do I call you servants, for a servant does not know what his master is doing; but I have called you friends, for all things that I heard from My Father I have made known to you.*

Proverbs 18:24*(nlt), "...but a real friend sticks closer than a brother."*

Deb Copenhaver, Casey Tibbs, Bill Linderman

Nothing But Bull

~~~

rowing up in the Spokane, Washington area, one of the big annual events was the Diamond Spur Rodeo. They competed on the football field at Joe Albi Stadium. Normally a portable panel is sufficient to contain bucking bulls and broncs. However, for whatever reason, for several years at least one bull would jump a panel and run amuck into the grandstand and the spectators. Whoopee! You've never seen chaos like this! Can you imagine a mean, panicked bull running wild through a grandstand of unsuspecting targets? Some were fleeing and others were being trampled. Incredible! The amazing thing was no one was ever killed or badly injured.

A few years ago I started having this dream on a somewhat regular basis. I would be at a rodeo arena and this brahma bull with huge horns would be after me. If I was in the grandstands, he would jump the fence and chase me just like at the Spokane rodeo. If I was up in the announcer's stand, he would begin to knock the posts over until the whole announcer's stand fell. In other words, one way or another, this bull was going to get me. I began to pray about this because I knew this dream wasn't from God. **II Tim 1:7** says, *"God has not given us a spirit of fear; but of power, love and a sound mind."* David said in **Psalms 34:4,** *"I sought the Lord and He heard me and delivered me from all my fears."* A Christian friend and I prayed one day and the Holy Spirit had us jump all over the fear operating against me in this dream. We knew at the end of our prayer that God had broken the torment that had been coming against me! Are you ready? That night I had the dream again. As usual here was the bull trying to kill me. He was in a corral with a big tall board fence. I was sitting on top of the fence looking down on him. All of a sudden I had no fear whatsoever and I jumped off the fence onto the bull. The moment I touched him, he turned into a shriveled up cowhide – nothing but a hide – dead, lifeless, powerless.

Satan is a bully – he has terrorized, deceived, tormented and lied to all mankind. Have you ever heard this definition of fear? F. - false E. - evidence A. - appearing R – real. The devil's agenda is to convince you that his negative garbage is real. David faced Goliath - that is all that God needed - someone to face up to the giant. What is tormenting you? What fear or fears is taking the joy out of your life and keeping you from launching into the life of a champion? You are God's champion! He lives in you. That fact gives you no reason whatsoever to fear anything on this planet; but God Himself. Do you recognize any of these bulls?

Fear of closed in spaces
Fear of snakes
Fear of spiders
Fear of heights
Fear of protection

Fear of lack
Fear of death
Fear of failure
Fear of rejection
Fear of man

And the list goes on and on and on.

In my dream, I took a leap of faith – that leap made a statement. It said, "I'm not afraid of you –I'm coming after you! I refuse to cower to you!" What's your leap of faith? I'm sure you know what it is. Are you afraid of what your friends would think of you if you received and served Jesus? Are you afraid to fly overseas on a mission trip? They're waiting for you. Are you afraid to start that new business? The originators of Starbucks coffee, Dell Computers, and Wendy's hamburgers were probably afraid too; but they took a leap of faith. Are you afraid of your husband who's been physically, mentally and verbally abusing you? Are you afraid to really pursue your dream? What if you fail? Hey – worse yet- what if you never try! Find a friend who can agree with you in prayer, and jump on that cowardly bull. Plus, get a "bull slaying" scripture, memorize it, study it and speak it till it becomes rich in your heart. Life's too good and too short to live it in fear!

Your giant is "nothing but bull."

GO FOR IT!

Isaiah 14:16, *(net)*, *"Those who see you (satan) will gaze at you and consider saying, "is this the man who made the earth tremble, who shook Kingdoms?"*

One of my Champion students.

Landon Koehn

"Favorite Scripture"
2 Tim.1:7 - God has not given me a spirit of fear but of power, love and a sound mind.

Advantages and Disadvantages

———❦———

*I*t was 1976 and something really special was taking place in the rodeo and calf roping world. Dallas Cowboys football star Walt Garrison and world champion roper Ernie Taylor came up with the idea of having a top 16 in the world match calf roping. It would be tournament style with two man matches, roping six calves in each match. First place was $15,000. That was a lot of money then. You could buy two nice trucks with that amount.

Two weeks before the event I was opening a power chute gate at a practice session in Aledo, Texas. I didn't realize as I pulled the lever on the gate with my right hand that my left hand was in harm's way. It cut off the end of my middle finger on my left hand. My roping buddy drove me to a hospital emergency room at about a hundred miles per hour. Then I told him my finger wasn't worth dying over. They operated on me and took skin off my forearm and sewed it on the end of my finger.

Now I had to make a decision. Could I possibly compete effectively roping this many calves with such a handicap? After talking to a doctor and getting a plan to put a guard over my finger; I decided to "go for it"! The first night came and I was matching a tough perennial NFR roper from Nebraska - John Rothwell. My focus wasn't on beating John as much as it was trying to tie each calf down with my new found challenge. Well to my surprise, I won the first match even though I had to slow down to negotiate my finger.

My next match was with Larry Cohorn, a tough New Mexico roper who rode a super hard stopping horse. I had a thought that day (probably a divine one) that Larry's horse would stop so hard that he would break a rope. Well, guess what? He did! I won my second match and now I was going to the semi-finals - roping against Gary Ledford an NFR roper from Oklahoma. On about my third calf (of six) the unthinkable happened! My calf kicked me in the finger and knocked off the entire transplant that had been sown on the end of my finger.

I had my doctor there just in case. He came out of the grandstands with his medical bag and (at the arena) gave me four shots of morphine painkiller - two on each side of my finger. Then he put gauze tape and an aluminum guard on it the best he could. It was time to rope. Well, I roped three more calves by the grace of God and another crazy thing happened! Gary and I tied to the tenth of a second. Now we have a two calf rope off. I was thankful to have survived six; now we rope two more. I had to be 8 seconds on my last calf and I was 8.6 and broke the barrier. Gary went on to rope against Roy Cooper in the finals. He beat Roy. Looking back, I had come within one tenth of a second to going to the finals under excruciating circumstances. I've looked back on that event and wondered why or how did I do that well at that competition.

I've been reading a book called David and Goliath. One of the chapters says there are advantages to disadvantages, and disadvantages to advantages. David seemed to be at a disadvantage because of Goliath's size; but it turned out to be just the opposite. Goliath was big and slow and the 125 lbs of armor he had on made him even slower. He was a sitting duck especially for a sling-shooting sniper like David. Goliath wanted David to enter hand to hand combat. David had a better idea.

Because of my injured finger, I had to slow down to execute the necessary steps of a roping run. Consistency is much more important in a match roping than speed. One of the things that seemed like a big disadvantage for me when I rodeoed was the lack of finances. It seemed an almost insurmountable disadvantage. However, many professional ropers I knew who did have money would quit and go home when the going got tough. When disappointments would overcome them they would say, "I don't have to put up with this, I'm going home."

Do you know that if Jesus Christ is your Lord and Savior that ultimately you have the advantage in life. Not only that but in Romans 8:28, " He promises to work all things (including disadvantages) together for good - for those who love God. If God be for us who (or what) can be against us." I could have chosen not to compete at the match roping that year and let the injury of the finger be my excuse. Instead I chose to face my giant and do what seemed to be impossible; and make my disadvantage be my advantage.

So, - big question for you! What are your advantages and disadvantages? Maybe things aren't as they appear. Could it be that your disadvantage is bringing the very best out in you? The courage, and the heart of a champion. A calf roper friend of mine's number one rodeo horse died. What a disadvantage. Wait! Another roper loaned him his two horses the next year and he went on to become the world champion!

Hey champion, get back in life's game to win - God truly wants you to win, to overcome every adverse circumstance.

GO FOR IT!

Romans 8:37(amp), *"Yet amid all these things we are more than conquerors and gain a surpassing victory through Him who loved us."*

SKOAL
Copenhagen

Roping Championship

By Jim Jennings

Back towards the last of March there was one of the greatest gatherings of professional calf ropers the world has ever seen. The occasion was the second annual Copenhagen-Skoal Calf Roping Championship, held in Fort Worth's old Northside Coliseum the 25th and 26th of the month. With all proceeds of the contest to go to the Lena Pope Home for children, 16 of the top calf ropers in the world were invited to vie for the $15,000 first-place purse, the largest winner's purse for any calf roping.

The contest was sponsored by U.S. Tobacco Co., makers of both Copenhagen and Skoal, and Louis Bantle, chairman of the board and president of the company, tells why they hold the event: "We've been involved with the National Intercollegiate Rodeo Association for three years now, and provide them with $100,000 a year in college fellowships. We were looking for further ways to develop a sport — rodeo — that we felt needed more promotion, and Walt Garrison came up with the

COPENHAGEN SKOAL CALF ROPING CHAMPIONSHIP 1977

U.S. Tobacco Co. officials, Walt Garrison, left, director of special events, and Louis Bantle, right, chairman of the board and president, congratulate Ledford following his win.

Old Fat Mare

Dad and I were telling rodeo stories the other night, and he told me about competing at a rodeo in Cranbrook, British Columbia. He had drawn a mare named Old Lady Clawson. Now, don't ask me why they named her Old Lady Clawson, but if I had to take a guess I'd say that Mrs. Clawson might have been a little bit on the mean side, or whoever named her didn't have a proper respect for the female gender. Anyway, she was kind of pot bellied and wasn't much to look at.

Not knowing anything about this bronc, my dad figured she probably wouldn't buck very much. It was almost time for the bronc riding to start and the stock contractor walked up to Dad and said, "I've got $10 that says this mare's gonna throw your backside out of the saddle." Dad said, "I'll call that bet and bet you another $10 that you've made a bad bet. In other words, let's make it $20." The bet was on!

Dad said when the chute gate opened he couldn't believe what a bucking horse he was on. He rode her to the whistle but it took everything he had to ride her. Here was the key though, Dad said if he hadn't bet the $20 he would have underestimated Old Lady Clawson; he probably would have bit the dust.

Satan can be just like Old Lady Clawson. He can look really harmless until the chute gate opens. Millions of people around the world watch pornography on the internet. It's just something you enjoy once in a while. What's the harm, right? Wrong! Seeds of pornography turn into crops of lust, marital discontent, divorce, rape, incest and every kind of perversion.

What harm can a little bit of marijuana or cocaine do? Everyone does it. Right? Wrong! I was at the Tarrant County courthouse in Ft. Worth, Texas as a character witness for a friend.

While I was waiting in the court room, I saw four separate cases of people, all in their twenties, sentenced to five years or more in the state penitentiary for doing drugs. One young man hugged his mother and aunt good-bye and began to weep. He had taken drugs for granted, he underestimated Old Lady Clawson and she bucked him off hard.

There's another side to the "Old Lady Clawson" principle. Many times in life we feel like the other guy got the gold mine and we got the shaft. Dad could have looked at the bucking chute next to him that had the super stallion bucking horse and said to himself, "Poor me, I drew life's "Old fat mare," no chance for me to win." You can't judge a book (or a mare) by its cover.

One of the most amazing achievements in rodeo and modern day sports history occurred from 1984 to 1993. Charmayne James incredibly won 10 world championships in a row in pro barrel racing. When you consider the multitudes of people who paid mega thousands for barrel horses in hopes of a world championship; yet no one could beat Charmayne's bay gelding named Scamper who had been bought at a feed lot in New Mexico for $1200.

Forget what someone else seems to be blessed with, just be content and faithful with what you have. One time the Holy Spirit spoke in my heart, *"Do what you can with what you've got, right where you're at."*

Dad won the bronc riding at Cranbrook that day, I believe, for two reasons: 1.) He didn't underestimate the situation, 2.) He made the best of the hand he was dealt. You can do the same and live a championship life.

GO FOR IT!

I Peter 5:8 *(nlp)*, *"Stay alert! Watch out for your great enemy, the devil. He prowls around like a roaring lion, looking for someone to devour.*

Squirt

⸎

It was October in Texas and I was having another month-long calf roping school. It had been a really hot summer (over 100 degrees) and we were hoping that by the first weekend of October things would cool down. Wrong! It was so hot that a couple of the students started to get sick as we were tying calves in the heat. We were taking a break this one particular day around two o'clock; and were heading for the water hose at the horse trough. We were thirsty - big time! Lo and behold one of the ropers from Saskatchewan, Canada was leading his horse up to us with a Squirt pop bottle in his hand.

Without hesitation a roper from Montana and I go running toward the Squirt bottle. He outruns me and grabs the bottle out of the guys hand and tips her up - glug - glug and then he begins to spit it out as I was grabbing the bottle from him. I remember saying "yeah right" to him thinking he was trying to keep me from enjoying a big swig of Squirt. Down she went. I chugged a big giant drink down; but it didn't get very far down and I launched it out violently. I ran to dunk my head in the horse water trough where Jim's head was already.

We would get a mouthful of water, spit it out and then repeat the process. What in the world had our soda pop heist gotten us into? What the heck was in that bottle? Well, at that time when you hauled horses across the Canadian border you had to have a test done on your horse. It was a lab test done on a horse's urine. Yes, you've got it! Plainly put - the Squirt pop bottle was full of horse pee - Yup! It's true! WOW! Awful would be an understatement. We couldn't believe it!

Have you ever done anything that stupid? Jim even tried to stop me and I wouldn't listen. You may wonder why I'm telling you this gross story. My encouragement for you is to beware of doing foolish things. If you're on planet earth and breathing, you're part of the human race. That means that you're capable of doing dumb stuff. Making mistakes is human (that's one thing), but making them continually puts you in a Bible category called "fools."

Proverbs talks a lot about fools. Jim and I definitely fit into that category that day. The dictionary defines fool as "a person who acts unwisely or imprudently - a silly person." Another definition is a person who lacks good sense or judgment. In **I Samuel 16** one of Saul's servants describes David (the giant killer) . . .he is a talented harp player, a brave warrior, a man of war, and has good judgment. This describes David just before he killed Goliath. He was a teenager and he already had good judgment.

Studying God's Word and then applying what it says to our life brings wisdom from heaven. In **Psalm 119** David said, *"Thy word have I hid in my heart that I might not sin against thee."* **James 1:5** says, *"If anyone lacks wisdom, let him ask of God, who gives to all liberally and without reproach, and it will be given to him."* I love to read Proverbs every day - 31 days in the month - 31 Proverbs. It's full of good everyday life tips that bring God's wisdom and good judgment into your life!

God wants you to have good judgment - champion. He has wisdom in His Word concerning all of life's scenarios. Don't be a fool - pray and think about life situations before you grab (that Squirt bottle) YUKK!

GO FOR IT!!

Prov. 12:15 *(God's Word translation) A stubborn fool considers his own way the right one; but a person who listens to advice is wise.*

Champions Don't Get In Offense (A fence)

I was talking to an angry young man in the 1980's at our Cowboy Church office at the Ft.Worth Stockyards. For an extended time he told me about someone that had done him wrong. As I responded to him, I made this statement: "you need to get your eyes on people's needs—to meet them, not on people's faults—to find them." Immediately after those words came out of my mouth, I realized they didn't come from me, but the Holy Spirit. This young man was seriously offended—he was caught in offense (a fence).

A couple of years ago we had a team roping school with a big jackpot at the end. One of the roping steers seemed to have a cow I.Q. of about three. He would try to get feed on the other side of the fence and ultimately get stuck in the sucker rods. It was no small chore trying to get his head back through the iron bars. We were worn out trying to free him; and the steer was going through some real pain.

Do you know someone who has been seriously offended? They are usually very angry people; just like the steer caught in the fence. They are mean to be around and they are a potential danger to others. It's like inviting a porcupine to a balloon festival. Proverbs 18:19 tells us, "a brother offended is harder to be won than a strong city; and their contentions are like the bars of a castle."

John Bevere wrote a book called, "The Bait of Satan" which is all about how and why people get caught in offense. Remember, offended people are angry, bitter people. Proverbs 9:8 says, "do not correct a scoffer (fool), lest he hate you; Here are three reasons why:

1. Bringing correction to a fool often brings offense. "Who are you to correct me?" Rebels and fools just don't take correction.
2. Jealousy. If someone is envious or jealous of what you have or what you've done, it doesn't matter what you do or don't do. They remain permanently offended just because of who you are.
3. Bitterness or unforgiveness. Being part of the human race qualifies all of us to be tempted to hangout in unforgiveness. Bob Hamp in his book, Think Differently, Live Differently says, "When we choose to forgive, we reclaim territory in our mind. As long as we are holding on to anger toward another, they own real estate in our mind."

Life situations that hurt us and wound us will keep our eyes on peoples' faults—to find them. How about you? Has someone done you wrong? Is your stance, "I'm going to make them pay—I hate them—I'll hurt them back?" Jesus said, "How can I forgive you, if you don't forgive others?" If you are a born-again believer, scripturally you cannot hold unforgiveness toward even one person and still make it to heaven. (Matt 6:14-15)

Here's a sobering story: A Navajo Indian lady from Arizona gave her testimony with an interpreter at Cowboy Church, Calgary, Alberta. She said her husband tried to kill her by driving both of them off of a cliff in Arizona. This happened close to their home. The husband was killed instantly and the lady crawled to the door of her house, and then died. She and her husband went immediately to hell. Neither one of them were actually surprised because they had both rejected Jesus while here on earth. What did shock them, however, was the presence of the pastor of the local church. The lady asked him, I know why I'm here but why are you here? He dropped his head and sadly said, "There was one person that I chose not to forgive." By the grace and mercy of God, the lady came back to life. She then received Jesus after her (hell) experience.

Now let's look at this statement again. "Get your eyes on

peoples needs to meet them—not on people's faults to find them." When we begin to do the first half then the second half seems to take care of itself. Acts 10:38 tells us that Jesus went everywhere doing good—meeting peoples' needs. When you do that you won't be looking for people's faults or shortcomings. You will begin to see with God's eyes of love.

Remember, champions don't get caught in offense (a fence).

Matthew 6:14 NLT *"If you forgive those who sin against you, your heavenly Father will forgive you."*

Second Chance

iva la Mexico! The year 2000 was a special experience for three other men and myself. We just finished a calf roping school in Saltillo, Mexico - 200 miles southwest of Laredo, Texas. The school was organized by our good friends Richard and Susanna Ashley, who have been missionaries to Mexico for many years.

The last day of the school was culminated by a matched competition - with prizes awarded to the winners. In the first competition we had two calves tied to two posts and we had two ropers run down the rope "dragster style" to flank and tie the calves. There was no stop watch, the first one to finish and throw his hands up won. In one of the pairings, a good roper named Hector, twisted his knee when he flanked his calf and was unable to continue. Unfortunately, that eliminated Hector from the competition; you could see the disappointment on his face.

As we continued on we ended up with an uneven number of contestants; only one cowboy at the end. We had to have two contestants, so I said, "Let's give Hector another chance since he twisted his knee the first time." Everyone agreed. Hector was rejuvenated, this time he won easily and qualified for the four man roping match. In the two head finals Hector "smoked'em." He won both go rounds and got the "goodies."

Something hit me like a hammer when I started thinking about that whole incident. **"Hector received a second chance."** One minute Hector was disappointed and eliminated from winning the prize. The next minute he was roping like a champion!

Everyone needs a second chance! No one is exempt from failure or difficulties. The greatest athletes, businessmen, scientists, or whoever made it because they got a second chance. Sometimes the person who needs to give you a second chance is yourself. No matter how bad you've messed up and feel like you don't deserve a second chance you need to get up and go again. This time you can do it! This time you can be the champion! This time happiness will be yours!

Have you fallen? Haven't we all. Get up and go again. **Proverbs 24:16,** *"A just man falls seven times and rises up again..."* The second chance principle will work for you just like it did for Hector. First Chance, the chump. Second chance, the champ.

After we awarded the prizes to the first and second place ropers we gathered all the ropers under a Mexican Mesquite tree. It was there that we told these Vaqueros something more precious than roping or rodeo tips. We shared what a change had come into our lives since we had received Jesus; God's second chance for the human race. **Romans 3:23**, *"All have sinned and come short of the glory of God."*

We were all born sinners according to the Word of God. We all have need of a savior. **John 3:3** reads, *"You must be born again."* Have you been born again? Have you received your second chance? If you have, or if you will, then just like Hector you can go from disappointment to experiencing God's love for you - "the goodies." He will lead you into a championship life now and forever.

IT'S NOT TOO LATE TO GO FOR IT!

Richard Ashley, Hector, Craig Sims
Saltillo, Mexico

Horse Thief

I was on my way to the Odessa, Texas rodeo; excited about the new rodeo year. Odessa and Denver were the first pro rodeos of the year (at that time). My teenage friend Ronnie and I pulled into a truck stop in Big Springs, Texas and unloaded my red roan horse "Little Joe." We tied him to the trailer in a parking lot some distance from the restaurant. After enjoying a good meal and a break from driving, we headed out to our rig. Little did we know that we were in for a "big surprise!" NO JOE! My horse was gone! My heart sank to my boots! The halter and lead rope were gone so I knew that he hadn't just broken free. Someone had taken him, a "Horse Thief." Guess what? Time to pray! What a privilege to be able to go to the great God of the universe who knows everything and is our very best friend. My young friend and I prayed and agreed that the Lord would help us get "Little Joe" back and in time to rope at Odessa. (**Matthew18:19**, "*Again I say to you that if two of you agree on earth concerning anything that they ask, it will be done for them by My Father in heaven*")

If you've ever been to Big Springs, Texas you know there is nothing but sagebrush and tumble weeds for miles and miles. We looked across the flats and had no idea which direction to begin our search. Then way out there a mile or more we saw a tiny cloud of dust on the horizon. It was our only shot. Off we went. We found a rabbit trail to drive on as our truck and trailer went bouncing and bucking across the Texas desert. Now, if this was a movie and you were watching, you would especially get a kick out of the young guy that was with me. He was riding shotgun in the seat next to me and I can guarantee you that he had never, I repeat never been in a situation as crazy as this one. His eyes were as big as saucers and he was stone silent. The closer we got - sure enough, we saw someone leading my horse on a dead run!

Now, you've got to know I'm not just mad, I'm not just excited, I'm ready to pulverize this guy. He stole my horse! In the old west they hung horse thieves. As we got closer, I hollered for the horse thief to stop and was surprised when he did. He turned around, faced up to me (and then a milli-second before I did {or said} something stupid), he began to cry. "I'm so sorry for taking your horse mister! All my life I wanted my own horse. I wasn't going to keep him - I just wanted to show him to my friends." As he began to speak, I could tell he was mentally challenged; he was taking my horse back to his home - a mental institution.

Wow! I just about started crying myself. Long story short, we didn't have a lot of time to spare - to get to the rodeo. But before we headed for the rodeo, we had to complete our new mission. Off we go to the mental institution to take "Little Joe" to see our horse thief's friends. He guides us to the dorm where he lives and here comes an army of younger guys who went wild over the horse. It's a good thing "Little Joe" was gentle because they were all over him. They were so happy and proud that their friend and new hero had found them a real horse. We let them pet on Joe as long as we possibly could before we loaded up. Pulling out of Big Springs with my rescued horse, I could barely believe this whole scenario!

A lot of things were swirling around in my mind. #1 - Jesus had answered our prayer to get my horse back. #2 - I was thankful that the Holy Spirit kept my anger in check long enough to let the young man speak first. That changed everything. **James 1:19, 20** says, *"So then, my beloved brethren, let every man be swift to hear, slow to speak, slow to anger; for the anger of man doesn't produce the righteousness of God."* #3 - It's great to be focused on our life's goals; however, events of that day showed us that we need to be flexible enough to recognize special moments that can change us and the lives of others.

Here's a word for you champion: Always pray first, stay calm (if possible) in life's storms, and be ready to reach out with the Love of Jesus!

GO FOR IT!

Prov. 17:27 "He who has knowledge spares his words, and a man of understanding is of a cool spirit."

John 13:34-35 (The Message), "Let me give you a new command: Love one another. In the same way I loved You, you love one another. This is how everyone will recognize that you are my disciples--when they see the love you have for each other."

Got my horse back, made it to the rodeo.

Little Things

Just A few years ago a champion team roper was competing at the big Feist team roping in Reno. It was the finals and his team was in the lead – in a position to win $100,000. He got a good start at the barrier and roped his steer in time to easily win first place. Just as he started off to the left with his heeler almost in position to throw, disaster struck. For no apparent reason his horse began to buck and buck hard. Needless to say they went out of the roping. Guess what had happened? The leather keeper that holds the back cinch in place broke and let the back cinch go up in the horse's flank and caused him to buck. What was the value of a leather keeper? Pennies, yet it was responsible for the loss of $100,000.

Song of Solomon says: *"it's the little foxes that spoil the vine."* Now, I'm not implying that things can't happen to anyone at a given time, but this story plainly illustrates why champions are so emphatic about dealing with details. I was always a fanatic about my ropes, strings, and tack. Everything had to be perfect. Experience (sometimes bad experiences) teaches you that if you're attempting to do anything with excellence, you have to tend to every little detail that you can.

I remember talking to my new students in Kansas and telling them that tie down roping is a 10,000 piece puzzle. That's a lot of little pieces, isn't it? World championships have been lost from a barrier that was broken by 1 inch or less. A bronc rider misses a horse out by the very smallest distance. It doesn't matter. I called the entry office two minutes late at San Antonio – one of the biggest PRCA rodeos in the country. The operator simply said, "I'm sorry sir, the entries have closed."

Isn't it the little things in our relationships; a look, a kind word, a gesture, a phone call, a word of encouragement at a key time in someone's life that can make such a difference? A tiny change in your business, your marriage, or in your God-given dream can bring forth the victory, the success, or the love you've been looking for. It would eternally benefit every person on the planet to read and study the Bible and then become determined to do all the big and little things it says to do.

The more we learn God's word, the more we can see all the intricate details that make up the incredible life He has for us. Make no mistake – champions in all walks of life tend to the little things.

GO FOR IT!

Song of Solomon 2:15, *"Catch for us the foxes, the little foxes that ruin the vineyards, our vineyards that are in bloom."*

Jeff riding Streak in the pacific ocean.

God's Good Horse

In the fall of 1973, I bought one of the very best roping horses in the country. His name was Streak. He cost $7,500.00, which was off the graph for what anyone had paid for a roping horse at that time. He was a Leo Bar-bred horse and was one of the best looking horses that I'd ever seen, a copper red sorrel. I was so tickled to own this horse that I could hardly contain myself.

I brushed him and brushed him. The more I brushed him, the more oil it brought to his coat and the more he would shine. His coat shone like a ray of sun reflecting off of a brand new copper penny. Little kids would always come running up to me and want to pet Streak. "Hey mister, that sure is a pretty horse, " they would say.

What I really liked about Streak was that he was as good in the arena as he was to look at. He was a ser-vant to me for many years - never griping never complaining. The Bible says that the reward for those that love God will be the Lord telling them *"well done good and faithful servant."* (**Matthew 25:21**)

Streak

I believe that God wants us to be His "good horse." Jesus wants us to shine just like Streak! Read these scriptures slowly and carefully. **Daniel 12:3** (Living Bible)" *And those who are wise - the people of God - shall shine as brightly as the sun's brilliance, and those who turn many to righteousness will glitter like stars forever."*

Philippians 2:14-15 (Living Bible), "*In everything you do, stay away from complaining and arguing, so that no one can speak a word against you. You are to live clean, innocent lives, as children of God in a dark world full of people who are crooked and stubborn. Shine out among them like beacon lights, holding out to them the Word of life.*"

Have you ever seen a horse with a bad coat of hair? The dead, colorless lifeless, grungy outside hair is a reflection of the poor health on the inside. It may be due to poor diet, worms, lack of exercise, or no TLC. Regardless of the reason, the result is no shine. Let's examine some of the things that can keep you from shining as God's good horse.

1. **Diet** - Are you feeding on God's Word? Jesus said, *"Man should not live by bread alone but by every word that proceeds out of the mouth of God!"* If your diet consists of rodeo papers, sports pages, and worldly input only, you are starving spiritually. Feed on the Bible daily, first.

2. **Worms** - Worms are hidden sins in your life. If you don't deal with them, they will eat you from the inside out. It could be pornography, sex outside of marriage, adultery, dishonesty, lying, laziness, jealousy of what someone else possesses or can do, greed, or indifference/luke warmness toward God. Whatever it is, wormy horses don't shine. Read **1 John 1:9** - Kill those worms!

3. **Lack of Exercise** - the apostle Paul said I have fought the good fight, I have run the race. Get running the race that God has for you. Quit sitting on the fence! Sweat a little, exercise brings shine!

4. **Lack of TLC** - Maybe you've never been treated very good or have a bad self image - you feel rejected. Perhaps you've never really been loved. God wants you to know how much He loves you. His love is unconditional; it's not based on your performance! He wants to "brush you." After you've received Jesus Christ, God wants you to know that you are loved, accepted, and forgiven. The past is over, and the new life ahead is an abundant, joyous life!

The more you brush a horse, the more inner oil it draws to his coat. God's oil is His anointing, which is His very presence. It is His glorious love. He wants that love to begin to shine in your life. Obedience to God's Word is allowing Jesus to brush you over and over. Become God's Good horse. Receive Jesus as your savior, then submit your life to His Lordship.

GO FOR IT!!

Isaiah 60:1-3, *"Arise, my People! Let your light shine for all the nations to see! For the glory of the Lord is streaming from you. Darkness as black as night shall cover all the peoples of the earth, but the glory of the Lord will shine from you. All nations will come to your light; mighty kings will come to see the glory of the Lord upon you.*

Cowgirl Hall of Fame

—⊶⊷—

My sister Debbie and I left our Northern Idaho home in Post Falls heading for a rodeo in Portland, Oregon. Debbie was driving with a permit, and I was riding "shot gun". She was fifteen years old and I was fourteen.

We're pulling horses and driving into some of the wildest traffic in the nation. I never told her how scared I was. How we survived that trip let alone made it to the rodeo only God knows. I don't remember if she placed in the barrel racing or if I did in the calf roping; but I do know that Debbie was my driving hero. Our great times rodeoing together came to a halt when our folks divorced. Debbie stayed with Mom and I lived with Dad.

It was 1974 and Debbie and I found ourselves together again in Seaside, Oregon. Her friend had purchased a beautiful horse facility there. It had an indoor arena and an outdoor arena. It was the perfect training camp for a calf roper. Debbie had told her friend about my dream to be a champion roper. 10,000 practice calves and three months later; the stage was set. Debbie decided to go with me and run barrels at all the big winter rodeos. We were on the rodeo trail together again – this time as young adults.

Sometimes life seems to have this incredible way of humbling you even when it looks like you have it all together. I was roping so good and my newly purchased horse (in my opinion) was the best in rodeo. We can't lose, right? Wrong!

Debbie was in the same boat with me—nothing seemed to click—no winnings. Overcoming the financial need for rooms, food, entry fees, fuel, etc, was gigantic. I roped my first calf at the last big opportunity of the winter—Houston, Texas. I didn't place —Debbie decided to go on to Phoenix where I would meet her later.

When Debbie left Houston, things couldn't have seemed much worse. But guess what? I qualified for the finals at Houston—won the short go and second in the average—WOW —rocket launched! We're back in the game to win. Get this, Debbie gets to Phoenix and while she was waiting for me, she visited a foundry in Prescott, Arizona where they cast bronze statues. It was then she realized what she wanted to pour her heart into. Debbie began to apply the same principles of success to her art career that had worked for her in rodeo. In Debbie's words:

"That day led to where I am today; a member of the National Sculpture Society and an honoree in the Cowgirl Hall of Fame. That one year was the turning point in each of our lives. Both Jeff and I are in a position to reflect on our lives and share with others the knowledge that through Jesus Christ all dreams are possible."

So where have life's travels brought you? You had big dreams, and it looked like there was no way you could lose. But you did; everything seemed to crumble in your hands. Maybe you ended up in financial ruin, divorce, prison, or incredibly discouraged.

If Jesus is your Lord, God is your partner. He is with you, for you, and He 'still' wants you to win. Keep going forward—one more step. I roped my next calf—Debbie drove to Arizona. In the midst of disappointment and discouragement, something great was truly around the next corner. Do you know that all God has to do to turn your life around for the good is give you one idea or one thought—one key person, or maybe—a champions devotional. There are a million things that can be the turning point in your life. The best is ahead for you. Let God help you turn a tough time into your victorious turning point. You are God's special Champion!!!

James 1:23: *Dear brothers and sisters, when troubles of any kind come your way consider it an opportunity for great joy. For you know that when your faith is tested your endurance has a chance to grow.*

Debbie Fellows,
Benny Binion,
and Billy Bob Barnett

Sit on Your Bucket and Relax

By Phil Doan

One day I headed out with the team and hay rack to feed about twenty head of saddle horses in a 40-acre pasture. It was a beautiful winter morning, the sun shining brightly on about three feet of fresh snow. It was one of those times that I was just thanking the Lord to be alive – not a care in the world. However, things were about to change!

I had some hay bales on the rack with several five-gallon pails of oats to feed the horses. About ten or twelve of the horses saw me coming and ran to the other side of the fence to me. I hurried to get the gate open and get the team and rack through before the horses could get to the gate. Once through, I stopped the team, threw the reins over the front of the rack, then ran back to shut the gate. About half of the saddle horses beat me to the open gate. I tried to stop them from going through the gate by yelling, "Whoa! Whoa!" while running with great difficulty through the deep snow. I was unsuccessful.

Things went from bad to worse. I looked back and my team had started to walk away on their own. I turned and started to run back through the deep snow to the rack and team, again yelling, "Whoa!" The harder I ran, the faster they ran. A pail of oats upset and fell off the rack. I grabbed it as I ran past. Right in the midst of all this I heard – way down in my heart – the Lord speak and say, "Why don't you relax?" I said, "I can't, that team is running away and it's going to wreck everything." They were running down a narrow trail between the fence and the trees.

Again, the Lord said, "Relax, sit down." I looked at the pail in my hand, turned it upside down, sat on it and said, "Okay, but I just know things are going to get wrecked." The Lord said, "Just relax." I replied, "Okay, it's your horses and harness and rack." As I sat there on my pail, I pulled out my little pocket

Bible and started to read. I could hear the team running through the deep snow and the tree branches hitting the rack. As I would start to get anxious again, I would hear, "Just relax." I thought, "Okay, but I just know everything will be a wreck."

As I forced myself to stay on the bucket, a great peace came over me. The horses ran completely around that forty acres between the fence and trees, came right up behind me as I sat on that bucket, and stopped about five feet away from me. Not one scratch was on the horses or the rack, not one piece of harness was broken. The reins were still draped over the front of the rack where I had thrown them. All the rest of the pails of oats were still on the rack. The only thing that had fallen off was the pail I was sitting on.

So, if you are going through a stormy time in your life and have become anxious about things, grab a bucket, sit on it and relax.

Just do it!

I Peter 5:7 (amp), *"Casting the whole of your care – all your anxieties, all your worries, all your concerns, once and for all – on Him; for He cares for you affectionately, and cares about you watchfully."*

**Phil Doan
Canadian Rodeo
Hall of Fame inductee**

Marlboro Man

A few years ago, I was tying calves with some of my students and I had 2 or 3 bloody places on my fingers and a rope burn on my wrist. I wound up with tape all over me. We tied for quite a while and as we stopped for a Bible study break, the Holy Spirit put this on my heart. "What is your faith costing you?" It was like He had me look at my arms and fingers and realize there is a "price to pay" for anything you're truly dedicated to, and want to excel at.

It was Pendleton Round-up Rodeo time in September of 1978. This picture of me was taken by an advertising agency that was hired by Marlboro Cigarettes to help them select two new Marlboro men.

Jeff at the 1978 Pendleton Roundup

Well, the short of the story is that I was one of two chosen. Just one month earlier I had quit smoking; a habit I'd had for about eight years. The Holy Spirit had been speaking in my heart "those cigarettes are killing you!"

When the Marlboro people finally contacted me I told them "I appreciate the offer, but I have just quit smoking.-- not only that, but I teach roping schools to a lot of young people, and I wouldn't want to influence them to smoke." The guy just about freaked out! He couldn't believe that I was turning him down. Did that cost me anything? Absolutely – maybe between $200,000 and $300,000 or more. It was a lot of money in 1978 - a lot today. But is that the end of the story? No way! Within six to twelve months my lungs were at 100%. I could go for a run and not feel any shortness of breath. In addition, a constant cough I had developed totally went away,

Financially, God met our needs and blessed us like only He can. - without the Marlboro money!. My question, "is money king in your life or is Jesus Lord?" If it's the latter then you will give your tithe (10%) and your offering to Christian churches and ministries that God leads you to. You will tell others (starting with your family and friends) about Jesus Christ. Will there be a price to pay? Yes sir! You will be mocked and made fun of. You'll be called things like: "a religious fanatic," "Bible thumper," "holy roller," and worse. But hang in there, don't panic, don't break and run; keep loving people and loving God.

My wife Sherry had eight party-girl friends when she gave her life to Jesus. At first she was the odd duck out. Then her friends began to see that what had happened to Sherry was real, and one by one they began to give their lives to Jesus until all eight were born again.

We're living in a day and time of fast foods, drive through convenience, and buy now – pay later plans. This generation has been trained to get it now. Too often, life is more about you than loving others. Your thoughts are about you - what you want -and when you want it.

Sex outside of marriage is no longer uncommon in the Christian world. Getting instant gratification is often a higher priority than getting to know who someone is. My encouragement to all of God's kids is this: Our savior and Lord said if He was persecuted and attacked, how much more will we be likewise. However, if we live like the world lives no one will know that we are the King's Kids. We can sin and fit in or walk straight and be great!

Recently a fifteen year old girl in Dallas, Texas found $2000 outside a bank. She decided to turn the money into the bank. After she turned in the money, they informed her they weren't giving it back to her. She could have kept it, but she told her dad that her conscience would not allow her to keep it. Now, here's the rest of the story. Someone heard about the girl on the news and sent her $3000. Someone else sent her $1000, and guess what – the bank decided to give her back the $2000. Because she decided to walk in God's principles of honesty and integrity, He blessed her (through people) with $6000. WOW!!

Champion, your walk will cost you something – but the rewards will be great here on earth and for eternity!

GO FOR IT!

Luke 9:23 (amp) *"And He said to all, if any person wills to come after Me, let him deny himself (disown himself, forget, lose sight of himself and his own interest, refuse and give up himself) and take up his cross daily and follow me (cleave steadfastly to Me, conform wholly to My example in living and, if need be, in dying also)*

"Being a witness to the next generation."

WELCOME TO "THE MASTER'S" CHAMPIONS

Champions Live With A Cause

It was the mid 1970's and the scene that was unfolding was unusual to say the least. Around 200 professional rodeo cowboys were all gathered together in a rodeo arena in the state of Washington. A steer wrestler friend of mine and myself had called this meeting to discuss striking. Yes, you heard right, a major PRCA rodeo. (In other words we were refusing to compete). For years we had cussed and discussed doing something about the lack of prize money in Pro rodeo. Finally, it was time to act.

As the discussion began, the looks on the cowboys' faces would convince anyone that this was nothing to take lightly. Everyone wanted better prize money, but not everyone wanted to risk their rodeo futures in the process. Thankfully, the fears we were experiencing were not equal to the courage and the inner resolve of knowing that our cause was an honorable one; and it was time to step out of the boat into the water. We all stuck together and that strike triggered this particular rodeo to add nearly three times the prize money within three years. It was a small victory in a big battle; but it was a step in the right direction.

In the story of David and Goliath in I Samuel 17, David came to the battlefield to bring his brothers some food, when Goliath came out to taunt and intimidate the army of Israel. David was immediately ready to battle with Goliath. The whole army of Israel was scared to death, and yet David was ready to rumble. Out of jealousy, David's brothers began to hurl accusations at him. In I Samuel 17:29, David told his brothers, "Is there not a cause?" David had a reason for living! In verse 46, he explained further what his cause was, "That all the world will know that there is a God in Israel!"

Aren't you glad our ancestors had the incredible courage to undertake a revolutionary war? Can you imagine this little up-start nation daring to defy England; which at that time was the most powerful nation on the face of the earth? Can you imagine facing an enemy firing line 75 feet in front of you; or enduring winters where many starved and froze to death? They kissed their wives and children goodbye knowing that this could likely be their last farewell. They lived and died for a cause, knowing that the real beneficiaries would be their children, their grand-children and the generations after!

I met Spud Tindell in July 2002. He brought his daughter Courtney to one of our Masters Champions Events in Spearfish, S.D. They drove all the way from Star, Mississippi. It began an incredible friendship. Spud was a full time rancher, a full time lineman for AT&T telephone company, and a missionary to the Ukraine, Africa, etc. He's been to the Ukraine alone 40 times. How does someone find the time or make the time to live sev-eral lives at once? There's only one answer - he lives with a "cause!"

Since 2002 Spud has come to our events all over North America (at his own expense). Yes, that's right! On top of ev-erything else he does, he takes time out of his life schedule to be a servant to this ministry. Spud and his wife Debbie are truly champions in Gods kingdom. They live with a cause bigger than what blesses their personal life, family, finances or friends. Their desire is - to see the kingdom of God expanded, to see oth-ers come to know and serve the Jesus that they love.

How about you - are you living with a "cause?" Completing what God has placed in your heart and fulfilling the plan that

He has for you is just as timely today for those around you as it was for those in Bible days. God uses people in all walks of life - cowboys, bankers, ranchers, lawyers, nurses, inmates, cattlemen, housewives, military men - living with a cause. Fulfilling that cause can bring our nation back to truth, righteousness and holiness; back to the Lord Jesus Christ. Are you ready to be all in?

GO FOR IT!

Phil.3:12 (nlt), *"I don't mean to say that I have already achieved these things or that I have already reached perfection. But I press on to possess that perfection for which Christ Jesus first possessed me."*

Mark 16:15, *"Go ye into all the world and preach the gospel to every creature."*

Spud and Debbie Tindell

Duck Your Heads, Boys

———— ⋙⋘ ————

*I*t was the mid 1950's and my dad (Deb Copenhaver) was working rodeos at Chicago, New York and Omaha. Once again he was flying with bareback rider and pilot Paul Templeton, Bill Linderman, and "Calgary" Bob Robinson. It seems crazy to say but if riding bucking horses isn't wild enough (often life-threatening), sometimes trying to get to the next rodeo is even worse. This story is an example ...

Paul was an Indiana Jones "cowboy style" pilot. You have to understand the typical rodeo mentality is: "one way or another we are going to get to the rodeo in time to compete!" Considering the possibilities of danger just doesn't seem to enter into the equation.

So off they go from New York to Omaha in a small single engine plane - a Cessna 180. They flew for a couple of hours and then had to land because fog was setting in. They sat at a small airport and waited for the weather to clear when Paul said, "We have to leave now if we're going to get to Omaha on time."They decide to go - a decision they would regret. They flew for a few minutes and then the worst thing happened. The fog thickened and they could see nothing. Paul said, "we've got to go down and see if we can find an opening." Down they go and Paul finds a river. He drops the plane close to the river flying just a few feet above the water. So here they are flying over a river with almost no visibility. I guess you could call it "dead men flying." They flew for several minutes when Paul shouts out something that chills these cowboys to their boots. "Duck your heads boys we're going under." There was barely room to clear the bridge and the water!

Two seconds later with their lives in the balance, they were on the other side - alive but still on the river. Dad said they flew for a few more minutes or so with little hope of surviving their predicament. Finally something appeared that was like heaven itself - a bright ray of light with an opening in the fog and clouds, Dad said he couldn't describe the feeling he had when the blue sky appeared! It was like the glory of God showered down on us. He said, "it was the most satisfying thing I'd ever seen in my life."He didn't mention angels or celestial music; but it would have fit the scenario! Off they went on to Omaha. I'm real sure though, that their thankfulness for being alive far outweighed what they did at Omaha. When Dad told me this story, I realized that it was a miracle (the grace of God) that I grew up having a dad.

It's something to realize that just one poor decision can be the difference between life and death. My Dad wasn't a Christian then; but I believe God was speaking to him saying, "Deb, when all hope seems gone and there seems to be nowhere to turn, I'm right here. I'm real and I'm the ray of light, the blue sky in your worst life situations."

I heard the song "Somewhere Over the Rainbow" the other day and thought of this plane story. Look at these lyrics: "Somewhere over the rainbow way up high; there's a land that I heard of once in a lullaby. Someday I'll wish upon a star, wake up where the clouds are far behind me; where trouble melts like lemon drops, high above the chimney tops; that's where you'll find me."

In dad's case, this song is not a myth or fantasy. When you know Jesus personally, He has a "Promised Land" for you. We can wish upon a star. Jesus is called the bright and morning star. With Him trouble will melt like lemon drops and life's clouds will be far behind you. Now trust Him - when there seems to be no hope or vision; and you have little or no faith. You may think you're going under - but blue skies are ahead!

My Dad had a great future ahead of him in rodeo - two world championships, Cowboy Hall of Fame, and Pro Rodeo Hall of Fame. However in the midst of this life threatening situation, a (death) fog appeared - it could've all been over before these good things could happen. My Dad didn't know the Lord then, but after this ordeal, he realized that there was a greater power who was in charge of life and death! Are you facing a difficult situation in your life? Maybe even life threatening. Use the name that is above every name: Jesus (**Phil 2:9-10**). When you speak it, it will take you under, over or around anything that would destroy you!

GO FOR IT!

Isaiah 43: 1-3 (message), *". . . Don't be afraid, I've redeemed you. I've called your name. You're mine. When you're in over your head, I'll be there with you. When you're in rough waters, you will not go down. When you're between a rock and a hard place, it won't be a dead end - because I am God, your personal God, the Holy of Israel, your savior. I paid a huge price for you. . . . ."*

Champions Live In Freedom

———— ∞∞∞ ————

*I*t was 1973 and I was flying into Williams Lake British Columbia with Harley May. Harley was not only a World Champion Steer Wrestler and President of the PRCA; but he was also a great pilot. We were working rodeos all over the country and as usual we were late. Harley flew us over the rodeo grounds and they were having the grand entry. Now, what does this mean? It means we're in big trouble because the grand entry will be followed by the bareback riding and then the calf roping.

We are several miles from the airport, we don't have anyone picking us up there, plus we have to get back to the rodeo grounds. Not only that, but the thought of "turning out" or not getting to compete after flying that far pushed me over the edge. I went into a frenzy of some kind and Harley looked at me and told me something that changed my approach to rodeo and life. He said: "Jeff, I figured out a long time ago that we can try hard to get there but if we don't make it, there will be another rodeo tomorrow. If we get there, great, if we don't, that'll be fine too."

Well, in the mean time we fly up to the airport, where there's only one car and it starts to drive away. Hall of Fame calf Roper Barry Burk is with us and shows us what to do when your only wheels are leaving. He literally jumped in front of the car and fortunately they slammed on the brakes. Barry told the couple, as we all jumped in, that we need to get to the rodeo – Pronto!!! Well, guess what? We made it – I don't remember if we won any money – but we got to compete.

The big thing for me though, was Harley's words rolling round and round inside me. 'If we make it, great, if we don't, that'll be all right too." The rest of that summer I simply enjoyed the journey. You know, life can be pretty sweet when we don't put ourselves in a pressure cooker of some kind. **I Peter 5:6-7** says, *"Therefore humble yourselves under the mighty hand of God, that He may exalt you in due time- -, casting all your care upon Him, for He cares for you."*

Did you know when you give your life to Jesus Christ that you have the God who created the universe living in you? He has all the power, creative ability and strength necessary to take care of you. Not only that but He has an unimaginable love for you. I believe that if we had any idea how much He loves us; we would melt like a pat of butter in a microwave.

That day flying into Williams Lake, I thought the world would end if I didn't get to compete. Think about that . . . are there things in this world that are possibly more important than our personal dreams, desires, schedules, quotas, goals? Maybe there are some things in your life that have been building up that have caused you to be hard to be around – in your marriage – your family – your school – your work place. Remember Harley's words: "if we get there great, if we don't, that will be fine too – there will be another rodeo tomorrow." When we commit it to God, then we can enjoy the journey!

GO FOR IT!!

Jeff at Oklahoma City 1984

Hidden In The Background

―――❦―――

Professional golfer, Tom Lehman, was ready to quit his golf dream. He had been pursuing it for some time and the breakthrough had not come. Finally, he told his wife that he was going to take a job at a well-known golf course as the club professional. Now, to many people that would have been a dream come true. However, that was not Tom's dream; his dream was to make it big on the PGA tour.

At the crucial moment, Tom's wife put her foot down and said, "we've come this far, we're not turning back now." She encouraged him to go on; somehow the family would get past the immediate financial giants. The rest is history. Tom went on to become the PGA tour player of the year – the highest honor in golf. He has won multi-millions in his career.

In 1975, a friend of mine flew to El Paso, Texas, to encourage me. I was under financial pressure and wanted to quit. My friend said, "Surely you didn't pay the price to get this far to quit now." Thank you so much Doug! Being raised in a rodeo family, I saw the support and sacrifice that Mom gave my Dad. Get this: my Mom drove from Northern Idaho to Ft. Worth, Texas, 2000 miles in a car, by herself pulling a one horse trailer with a horse in it. My sister and I were babies then; not only that, it was the dead of winter and she fought snow storms to make it. Wow! What a champion!

Another year my Dad was heading for Denver, the first big winter rodeo; funds were scarce at the time, and Dad didn't want to take the little money we had and use it for entry fees and traveling expenses. Much like Tom Lehman's wife, my

Mom told Dad to get going; "we'll be just fine." He went, and he won! Praise God for champion women!

The greatest champions many times are not even visible to this world. They are behind the scenes, often paying the biggest prices, making the biggest sacrifices, yet with little or no recognition or applause. It could be your encouragement that makes all the difference for someone who is about to give up on their dream. Maybe the world never acknowledges you, but God sees you and knows.

CHAMPION –
YOUR ENCOURAGEMENT IN THE BACK-
GROUND IS SEEN AND REWARDED BY GOD!

Prov. 31:10-11, *(the message), "A good woman is hard to find, and worth far more than diamonds. Her husband trusts her without reserve, and never has reason to regret it."*

Deb Copenhaver and my mom Leslie.

Deadly Company

A couple of years ago, my 20 year-old friend started running with a bad crowd. He was a born-again Christian; but he got in with the wrong crowd. Pretty soon he was involved in some petty theft and then a convenience store robbery. It's probable at that point that he was trying to break free from the group, but one of his so-called "friends" decided they wanted to take his car and leave Texas. The ring leader, who was only 17 years old, walked up to my friend, pointed a stolen .357 magnum pistol point blank in his face, asked him if he had ever seen one of these and then pulled the trigger. My young friend fell face down to the ground and then the guy shot him again in the back of the head. How does someone end up in a situation like this? Listen to these scriptures in the first chapter of Proverbs and you will know.

Proverbs 1:10-16 (Liv. Bible), *"If young toughs tell you, come and join us – turn your back on them. We'll hide and rob and kill, they say. Good or bad, we'll treat them all alike and the loot we'll get! All kinds of stuff. Come on; throw in your lot with us. We'll split with you in equal shares. Don't do it son! Stay far from men like that, for crime is their way of life and murder is their specialty."*

I did his funeral in the courtyard at Cowboy Church. It was very sad. He was a good young man, he knew the Lord; and yet he got in with the wrong crowd. I believe at this point he wanted to break free from these guys; but he was afraid to face up to them and their plans.

Proverbs 29:25, *"The fear of man brings a snare."* A snare is a trap that after you've stepped into it, without the intervention of God, you won't go free. Now, I can't prove this next statement, but I believe nonetheless that it's true. I believe that more people will end up in hell because of the inability to overcome the fear of man; what others may think, or what they think others may think about them. (1) Drug friends will lead you on into crime, divorce, financial ruin, and a life of destruction. (2) Partying, drinking, carousing friends will always lead you away from God.

A more subtle danger, but just as deadly, are those who are apathetic, lukewarm, and indifferent about Jesus and the things of God. They'll steal your joy, zeal, and excitement and pretty soon you'll wonder why God seems so distant. Or maybe your friends are just too cool for God. Part of the price you pay to be their friend is to never say anything about God, or admit that you have a desire to know God better. Let your light so shine brightly, (**Matt. 5:16**) and you'll find out quickly who your friends are! Now, I'm not saying to have a "holier than thou" attitude around your friends and act like you're better than them because you're a Christian. No, you need to pray for them and maintain that friendship as much as you can without compromising your walk with God. Hey champion, who are you hanging out with?

My wife is from Alberta, Canada. She had eight close friends when she became a Christian. At first, they stayed away from her; but one by one they began to come to the Lord, when they saw the change in Sherry's life. Eventually all eight of them were saved. I repeat, all eight came to the Lord. Sherry may have seemed a little weird to them (for a season); but as time went on her friends could see what she had found was real. Remember, Jesus said, *"If you confess me to others, I will confess you to the Father. If you deny me before others, I will deny you before my Father."*

Tell your friends the truth, pray for them, and then "walk the walk" in front of them. Don't play in the pigpen of their sin with them. Do you want to be happy, really? I mean for real, or do you want to be a Christian that's always afraid to take a stand for God around your friends? Be a lion, live fearless, free from the fear of man. So what if people think you're peculiar. They thought David was peculiar to think he could whip a giant. They thought Jesus was peculiar. They thought his disciples were peculiar. Champions are peculiar. They're different – unique. **I Peter 2:9** (niv), *"But you are a chosen people, a royal* priesthood, a holy nation, God's special possession, that you may declare the praises of Him who called you out of darkness into His wonderful light."

Call on God to be your strength; call on Him to help you take a stand and live a life that's free from the fear of what others may say, or think about you. Be a giant-killer-champion!

God Wants You to Win!

I Cor. 15:33 *(tlb)*, *"Bad company corrupts good morals."*

Sherry Copenhaver and Hope Vasquez
"Tom Mix and Tex Mex"

Rent A Paint

*I*t was the early 1980's, and I found myself coaching month-long calf roping schools at my home in Granbury, Texas. The biggest challenge for the students when they came for that long was having enough "horse power." We were always trying to buy or rent or borrow extra horses.

The problem in calf roping is that basically no one wants you to ride their horse because they could get crippled or you could teach them a bad habit! So for the most part, the only option was to buy, and the guys couldn't afford that! But wait! A friend of mine found two paint horses in Ft Worth that we could rent. He said they were supposed to be pretty nice horses. Our guys were pumped! More horses meant getting to rope more calves! Big Fun! right? Well, here we go - "rent a paint!"

Wayne Warkentin a tough young calf roper from Manitoba Canada got on the first paint and was on his way (full speed) to his calf. At the very moment he was about to throw his rope - leaning forward in the front of his saddle, paint #1 decides he's going to do his impersonation of "Trade Winds" (a former bucking horse of the year). Now, if this would have happened to my dad who was a great bronc rider, that's one thing; but calf ropers aren't usually gifted in this area, let alone expecting a bucking explosion!

This paint horse stuck his front feet in the ground and threw Wayne in the air higher than I'd ever seen anyone launched off a horse; he sent him into a 360 degree spin in mid air. As all of us watched this unfold, we were stone silent. For a moment Wayne just lay there and then thankfully he began to stand up. WOW! When we could see he wasn't hurt, we started laughing so hard I thought we were going to injure ourselves.

Now, we have rent a paint #2. Because of the antics of paint #1, I decided I would ride paint #2 in case there was "Houston, we have another problem." Well, everything seemed to be going well. I roped this calf along the fence, my horse stopped and I got off - no paint problem, right? Uh - maybe not! Half way down the rope I heard an unusual sound. I couldn't figure it out at first; and then it dawned on me. I hear a thundering sound! Rent a paint #2 is about to run over me. I dive toward the fence and by a split second, avoid being stampeded! Paint #2 is on a dead run with the calf attached to him on the end of the rope. We all ran to the end of the arena and cut the rope - ending the second Rent a Paint drama!

That day our little ropers group learned a classic lesson. We presumed what we had been told was the truth about our paint friends. Boy, was that wrong. **Psalm 19:13 (nkjv)**, King David said, *"Lord keep back your servant from presumptuous sins; Let them not have dominion over me."* Presumption is presuming you know something when you truly know nothing at all. The opposite of presumption is truth. Jesus is the truth. He carries wisdom, knowledge and understanding in His Word. Our paint story is laughable, however someone could have been killed or paralyzed for life. We presumed we knew - what we needed was the truth.

Are you presuming you're going to heaven? After all, you're a good person - good people go to heaven, right? This paint doesn't buck - right? - wrong! Jesus said in **John 14:6 (nkjv),** *"I am the way, the truth, and the life. No one comes to the Father except through Me."* OK champion, don't let those "presumption paints" buck you off or run over you. God wants you to win!

GO FOR IT!

John 8:32 *(amp)*, *"And you will know the Truth, and the Truth will set you free. "*

Think Zone — Play Zone

I was reading a golf book the other day written by hall of fame golfer Annika Sorenstam. I love to study golf techniques to help me be a better roping coach. Here's an incredible tip that can help you in any sport or life itself. As Annika stands behind the ball, she looks at her target, considers the wind, the lie of the land, the position of the pin and any other influencing factors. As she begins to walk toward the ball, she crosses an imaginary zone she calls the *think zone*. She now steps into the *play zone*, where there is no more thinking and analyzing. The play zone means "let's rock." Let's do it!

I tell ropers the *think zone* is when you're on your horse outside of the roping box preparing to ride in. This is where you swing your rope making sure it feels right. You get your mind right, preparing for a great performance. When you ride your horse into the box and they hook the barrier behind you. . partner, you just left the think zone. Now, it's no fear, no tentativeness, no considering who's watching you. No thoughts of "what if I fail?" or can I win? None of that. You are now locked and loaded. You are the bullet in the chamber. . .you're in the *rope zone!*

Consider a UFC fighter getting into the cage. He might be the nicest, mildest-mannered Boy Scout troop leader outside in the think zone; but when he steps into the cage, the play zone - he's fearless and focused! Let's apply this to our walk with God. **Proverbs 3:5** says; *"trust in the Lord with all your heart and lean not to your own understanding."* There's a time to think, analyze, plan and ponder all aspects of something; then it's time to step into the play zone - the faith zone – trust in the preparation and then – do it!

II Kings, 7:3 tells the story of 4 lepers who were starving to death and condemned to die with leprosy. Finally one of them decided to step into the faith zone. He said *"why should we sit here until we die. Let's go into the enemy camp. The worst thing that can happen is they'll kill us; but we're about to die anyway."* Well, if you've read the story you know that the minute they took "steps of faith," the Lord made their steps sound like a mighty army. When they got into the enemy's camp it was deserted. They stepped into victory because they entered the "faith zone." Here's a tip! If we stay in the think zone too long, it could be a sign that our enemy of fear has paralyzed us.

Remember 9/11/2001: and the jet about to fly into the pentagon? One of the heroes on board called his wife and told her that he loved her. He then told his friends who were confronting the terrorists with him, "Let's roll." They stepped into the faith zone. Are you seeing it? No looking back, no second thoughts, no fear, no yesterdays, no tomorrow - only right now!

Step into the Faith Zone and Win!

Matthew 14:29 *(NIV), "Come," he said. Then Peter got down out of the boat, walked on the water and came toward Jesus.*

Deb thinking at Toppenish

Elvis Bling Cowboy

Nearly every spring and early summer my wife Sherry and I would rodeo in Alberta, Canada. Sherry is an excellent seamstress and clothes designer. She decided to start making fancy western shirts for people in the rodeo business. It was the early eighties in the time of afro hair-dos and bell bottom pants - not to mention polyester! Help! John Travolta, the Bee Gees, and *Saturday Night Fever*" were influencing even the cowboy world.

Sherry had a fashion show in Calgary with different cowboys and cowgirls wearing her custom shirts. Her shirt styles varied from fairly conservative to major bling! I was one of the models and my shirt was a gold and black shiny satin shirt with gold sequins and gold fringe. I don't know if Sherry thought that I was secretly an Elvis "wanna be," or maybe she wanted to stretch my "limited star image." On a bling scale of 1 to 10 this was a 17. The good news is that I made it through the fashion show and now I won't wear it again, right? "uh" wrong. Sherry decides she wants me to compete in it at the Lethbridge, Alberta rodeo. I immediately exercise my manly authority and tell her this isn't happening. I can't rope with long fringe on my shirt. It could get caught in the piggin' string when I'm tying my calf! Not only that, I'm just not liberated enough to wear an Elvis shirt at a rodeo. If you've been happily married for some time you probably already know where this part of the story is going. Off I go to the rodeo in my bling-bling. Yes, I love my wife! - a lot!

OK, here's the deal! If you wear a shirt like this in front of all these spectators and your peers, you only have one option – WIN! Anything short of winning would be an embarrassing disaster. You can't believe how self-conscious I was as I rode into the arena to compete. On the outside I was pretending to be cool, but on the inside I was saying, *"Lord, if I've ever needed some help, it would be right now."*

Here we go. I catch up to my calf and rope him around the top of the head – Oh no!- a miss – but wait. The end of the calf's foot (his dew claw) gets hung up with the rope around the top of his head. Ordinarily I wouldn't have even gotten off of my horse knowing the rope was going to pop off. I guess I dismounted in faith because when I got to the calf the rope was still holding the calf. I've roped thousands of calves in my life - in practice and competition; and not once did this ever happen. The calf had no horns - there was nothing to keep the rope on the top of the calf's head. I was personally witnessing a miracle; however I didn't have time to spectate. I tied the calf in 9.0 seconds and won the rodeo. To this day I've never seen anything like it. All I can say is only God could do it! I know that He helped me in a special way. So, did I start wearing bling shirts after that? UH, NO! I did wear Sherry's more conservative ones, however.

Have you ever been in a special life situation that you needed (I repeat) needed God to come through for you? Do you know that He wants to? Scripture says: *"Is there anything too hard for me?-says the Lord?* God can do anything – you just need to ask Him – out of the depths of your heart. Tell the Lord, *"Lord, I need you to be with me in a special way today."* Maybe you are in the middle of che-motherapy, or a divorce, or the biggest ball game of your life! It doesn't matter. Jesus is so wonderful, so powerful, so glorious, and so in love with all His kids. He's there for the asking!

James 4:2 says, *"You have not because you ask not. Ask that your joy may be full."* Maybe you are going to interview for the job of your dreams. Say, *"Lord I need you!"* He will be with you because

He loves you so much. You are His champion and He wants you to WIN!

GO FOR IT!

Isaiah 41:10 *(amp)*, *"Fear not, for I am with you; do not look around you in terror and be dis-mayed, for I am your God. I will strengthen and harden you to difficulties, yes, I will hold you up and retain you with My vic-torious right hand of rightness and justice.*

Jeff wearing his Elvis bling.

Champions Seek After God's Word

*couple of months after I gave my life to Jesus, I was at a church service in Ft. Worth, TX. That night the Holy Spirit spoke in my heart and said, "I want you to make your Bible the precious possession that your rope can has always been." Boy, God knows how to speak to a calf roper! For years rodeoing, I had always been a fanatic about having super good ropes and strings, not to mention that I kept my checkbook, spurs and other valuables in my rope can. I began to go for God's Word like I had roped calves. I realized the Bible is God's practice pen.

Listen to **II Timothy 2:15**, *"Study to show yourself approved unto God - a workman who needs not to be ashamed, rightly dividing the Word of truth."* The roper who doesn't practice or study his sport will be ashamed. The same with the Christian. If you don't read and practice what the Word says, life will bring much shame and embarrassment. Why, because His Word is the truth, it is His winner's manual for life.

Did you know the Word of God is His personal love-letter to you? Every day as you open it, read it, and do it you are eating the bread of life. **Matthew 4:4,** *"Man does not live by bread alone, but by every word that proceeds out of the mouth of God."* Memorize the Word, Champion, learn the principles that it's stories and scriptures teach.

In the "God Wants You To Have The Best Equipment" article, I talked about the things that happened to Sherry and me when we received the baptism of the Holy Spirit. One of them was the incredible desire to read, study, memorize and generally learn about God's Word, the Bible. Scripture talks about revelation knowledge; which is what happens when the Holy Spirit brings light or understanding to a certain scripture.

It's just like spending time in the practice arena. You're practicing every day and then all of a sudden you make a major breakthrough in your speed or consistency. On the inside the light goes on and changes everything! In **Ephesians 1:18**, the apostle Paul is praying the eyes of our understanding be enlightened - when that happens you'll never be the same. again.

The Holy Spirit loves to reveal Jesus (who is the Word) to us. Championships may appear to be won at The National Finals Rodeo in Las Vegas, but the truth is the practice pen is where it all takes place first. Likewise in life the Word of God and faith in the Word is where life's victories are won in advance.

REMEMBER CHAMPION - GOD'S WORD - THE PRACTICE PEN IS WHERE YOU WIN.

GO FOR IT!

John 1:1, *"In the beginning was the Word, and the Word was with God, and the Word was God."*

John 1:14, *"And the Word became flesh and dwelt among us and we beheld His glory, the glory as the only begotten of the Father, full of grace and truth."*

Hey champ, here are some power scriptures to study and learn:

II Tim. 1:7 (amp)	Heb 4:16 (amp)
Phil 4:13 (amp)	Eph. 2:8-10 (amp)
Prov. 24:3 (living)	Matt. 5:1-12 (message)
Hab. 2:2-3 (amp)	Prov. 16:3 (amp)
I Cor. 13:4-8 (amp)	I Cor. 12:9-10 (amp)
Eph 3:17-20 (amp)	Matt. 6:31-34 (amp)

The Big Three

I was in the 9th grade and really excited about playing football. It was my first love. As I remember, I weighed about 160 lbs, which was about average for our team. One of the major moments for our players at that time was the opposing team pulling up in their bus.

As they were stepping off, it was like gladiators on parade. When a 200 lb plus guy got off, you knew you were going to have to muster up a new kind of courage. On this one particular day, about half the players of the other team had gotten off their bus and then I saw something crazy! You may not believe this, but it's true. This guy was stepping off the bus - sideways! Why? Because he was too big to fit through the door front ways. I'm serious, every step he took - the front of the bus was rocking! He had to weigh 450 lbs. or more. He looked like the incredible hulk in football gear. They say a picture is worth a thousand words. I believe it! Words flashed through my mind like: smashed, demolished, flattened, etc. The good news for our team is that he was too slow to do all those things; but he was definitely intimidating. We managed to stay clear of him and won the game!

Well, years later I was thinking about that guy getting off the bus sideways and I saw a picture of what God is like when He comes to town! I saw this team school bus that you see pictured here. THE BIG THREE. Did you know that the Lord our God is One God; and yet the Bible says there are three persons? 1. God the Father 2. God the Son 3. God the Holy Spirit. God almighty created our planet and all the incredible creation on it. He split the red sea while His people walked across on dry land. He resurrected a man after the man had been dead for 4 days. He's a miracle God!

So what's up in your life? Do you have big obstacles to overcome? Some big needs? It's not unusual to weigh 160 lbs and have a 500 lb. life challenge present itself. No problem! God is more than enough. He comes with power and great authority. He is the great I AM. Describing Himself to Moses, God said to tell them that "I AM THAT I AM" sent you! Sounds like "THE MAN" doesn't it?!

I was reading **Psalms 23** in the amplified Bible one morning. The first verse says, "The Lord is my shepherd, to feed, guide, and shield me." "The BIG THREE" can guarantee your life's provision, guidance and protection.

Hey, check it out! The bus just pulled up. The door opens, 'The Big Three' are in town! They're steppin' off the bus - sideways! Here for you - stepping onto the field of your life with the power to change things on your behalf!

"THE BIG THREE"
BRINGING VICTORY - GOD WANTS YOU TO WIN!

I John 5:7 *(amp), "So there are three witnesses in heaven; the Father, the Word and the Holy Spirit, and these three are one!"*

The Perfect Setting

※

I was nine years old and entered in the steer riding at the Calgary Stampede. Wayne Vold, son of famed stock contractor Harry Vold won the steer riding that year; he was something special. I bucked off both of my steers fairly soon as I remember – probably my confirmation to rope calves. On a brighter note my dad drew a horse named Blue mountain in the finals at Calgary. It was 1958 but I can remember it like it was last week. Blue Mountain had thrown Dad off about a month prior to Calgary - boy, could he buck! Now, a rematch. Dad on Blue Mountain in the finals at Calgary - the *Perfect Setting!*

I had seen it many times before. A great rider draws a great horse or a great bull. Now, it's showdown time! Jim Shoulders gets on Blue Smoke at Nampa, Idaho; Dad on Miss Klamath at Ellenburg, Wash. – she'd never been ridden at that time. Calf roper Dean Oliver or Cody Ohl in the last round at the NFR, the short go at Cheyenne. It's all on the line. It seems the whole world is watching; it's the perfect setting!

Did you know that God sees your life from beginning to end? He knows the gifts, talents, strengths, and abilities in you because He placed them there.

Isn't it amazing to think we would never truly see the greatness of God in someone's life unless they are put in a special setting to reveal that greatness? I can remember clearly that same year in 1958, when Johnny Unitas was playing in the NFL Championship game - later tagged the greatest game ever played. And here was Unitas, one of the greatest quarterbacks of all time showing his stuff!

We saw policeman and fireman showing their greatness at the burning twin towers; soldiers in the armed forces in two world wars –Korea and Vietnam- laying their lives down for others. How would we see the brilliance of God's stones unless they're placed in the perfect setting! The preparation and training that you've been going through will not be wasted or frustrated if you will continue to trust Him and be persistent to wait for His timing. God holds the universe in His hands, and if your heart longs to glorify Him and to lift Him up – He will prepare the setting for you!

Back to the bronc, Blue Mountain. My Dad isn't a large man, but he seemed like a giant to me as he stepped over the chute on a "sure-nuff buckin' horse." The gate opened. Blue Mountain was jumping and kicking hard and changing directions on nearly every jump. Dad got the whistle; and the crowd went wild! It was his third time to win Calgary.

Maybe your life has left you wondering if your time will come; if your moment on Blue Mountain will ever manifest. Here's a key – as a boy Dad was getting on horses in a round pen at a sale barn in Davenport, Washington full of mud and manure. He was preparing for the future. We never know what God has in store for the future; but we can know that it will be good and worth the time, effort, and –sometimes - the agony of preparation. Stay under the Masters oversight; trust Him; especially when you don't understand. He loves you and He loves to show His kids off. "The stage is set". . . you're stepping over the chute – in your God-given dream!

It's the Perfect Setting! You're sparkling like a diamond champion!

GO FOR IT!

Matt. 13:43 *(asv), "Then shall the righteous shine forth as the sun in the Kingdom of their Father."*

Deb at Cheyenne

De-Sire

I n 2010 my dad received an award from the American Quarter Horse Association for fifty years of raising quarter horses. Some people like horses, some really like them and some love them. The latter would be my dad. He can name pedigrees of horse breeding like you can't imagine. He goes down the sires and dams of horses' pedigrees as fast as your big dog eats a pork chop. My dad has a stallion named King. King is almost twenty years old and has been a great performance horse producer for many years now. He puts a special stamp on all his colts, great dispositions, intelligence, confirmation, athletic ability and a desire to please their master.

I found out an amazing bit of information the other day. Did you know what the word desire means? "de" means "the" and "sire" means "father." Where do your unique God-given desires come from? The Father! Where does the desire to use your gifting, abilities and resources to glorify Him come from? Yes, they come from Him. Who's putting that fire – that creativity, that new invention – that world changing idea in you? It's coming from above - the stamp of God. Look at **James 1:17**, "*Every good and perfect gift comes down from the Father above…*" God places incredible heavenly gifts in us and then He ignites them with fire. It's called "desire" and it comes from the Father.

The enemy is a liar. One of his most effective lies is that if you really give your life, - your heart to God, life wouldn't be as fun; the Lord would take away the things that you truly love. Wrong – Big Time Lie! The truth is just the opposite. To fall in love with Him is to open the doors of your heart wide open, and let God fill you with desire fire. WOW! Don't run from Him, run to Him.

I went to a golf tournament the other day and was on a golf cart with a man who loves to hunt and fish. He told me he had just gotten back from a ten day African hunt. It was a dream (come true) trip for him. He is a Christian and he told me how God supernaturally made the way financially possible for him to be there. While he was there he got to share the Lord with the owner of the hunting lodge. It changed the man's life! I told my new friend that (similar to his hunting trip), I had just gotten back from teaching a calf roping school in New Mexico.

I have so much fun training young roping champions; and while I was there, I got to share my love for the Lord with the students and their parents. Here's a word for men: God doesn't take the fun out of life! He is the fun – He is the life – He is the joy. Are there things in your life that you have an incredible love for? Love God #1 – then do what you love to do and be His vessel. God wants you to be His blessing to others right where you are; because He put you there. Don't believe the devil's lies anymore – tell him to shut up and leave you in Jesus' name. Let the de-sires in your heart draw you to Jesus and what He has for you.

Champion - victory comes from De-Sire!

Psalms 37:4 *(nlt)*, *"Take delight in the Lord, and he will give you your heart's desire."*

P.S. My dad has touched the hearts of so many people through the years by giving them one of his horses. His de-sire to raise outstanding horses and bless others, has truly become a ministry.

Deb at Ellensburg, Washington

Eddie Bush

My bronc rider friend Eddie Bush used to live in Weatherford, Texas. His home was on a major highway. One of his pet peeves was people throwing beer bottles all over his property as they go merrily down the road. The litter slogan in the Lone Star State is: Don't mess with Texas." Eddie thinks "Don't mess with Eddie" would be better. One of Eddie's ongoing projects was to get his feed sack and walk down the front of his property on the highway and pick up bottles. Well, as the story goes, one day the word gets back to Eddie that someone (in his church) saw Eddie staggering down the road in a drunken stupor (with all these beer bottles). What? Eddie doesn't drink.

Someone tells him who the lady is that passed on "the drunken Eddie story." One Sunday morning after church Eddie walks up to the lady and says, "You know the story about me walking alongside the highway in a drunken stupor?" She stammered uncomfortably "Yes" and Eddie said, "Well, it's much worse than you think." Then he walked away. Isn't that the coolest?! Instead of defending himself and telling the lady how ugly it was to spread such an ugly, untrue rumor about him, he hinted that it was really more serious than she could imagine.

Have you ever had someone spread ugly rumors about you? Perhaps they told a story about you that didn't tell the other half of the story? I saw a saying on a sugar package at a restaurant one time. It said "don't explain - your friends don't need it and your enemies won't believe it anyway." People can have many reasons for disliking someone. Maybe they're jealous of something someone else has or has accomplished. Perhaps something happened that brought shame, humiliation, or both to their lives; and now the only consolation for them is to take it out on someone else. As born again Christians, Jesus has commanded us to forgive others just like He forgave us. Matthew 6:12, *"Forgive our trespasses as we forgive those who have trespassed against us."*

In **Philippians 4:8**, the apostle Paul tells us: *"Finally, brethren, whatsoever things are true, whatsoever things are honest, whatsoever things are just, whatsoever things are pure, whatsoever things are* *lovely, whatsoever things are of good report; if there be any virtue, and if there be any praise, think on these things.*

Gossip is sweet to those who are looking for something or someone to criticize or find fault with. The gospel is good news for man. Gossip is bad news about men. Only the devil himself working in and through someone could find enjoyment in destroying or diminishing another's worth. Never the less, Jesus said, "In this world you'll have tribulations; but be of good cheer for I have overcome them." Did anyone ever speak evil of Jesus? OH, YEAH! Pilate said to Him, "Are you the king of the Jews?" Jesus could have defended himself and possibly set himself free. He wouldn't do it! He didn't live to be seen in a better light before men. He also didn't care how many slanderous ugly words were shot at Him to destroy Him and the plan that God had for Him to fulfill.

Let me say this; it's a waste of time to even care what negative people think of you much less what they say about you. You make mistakes; I make mistakes. When we do (as Christians) we go to God for forgiveness. Then we walk forward by faith. Jesus walked in a higher realm than what people thought of Him. His goal was to obey His heavenly Father; walking in a realm higher than the opinions and attacks of men! That should be ours too!

In a court room the prosecuting attorney's job is to attack the person on trial with slander, criticism, verbal abuse, and character assassination; casting a shadow of guilt on the defendant. One of satan's names is "the accuser of the brethren." He attacks God's people through people on earth that he uses. Sadly, many of the people he uses are Christians. Christians attacking Christians - actually partnering with the devil! When soldiers shoot their own men it's called friendly fire. It's deadly and so sad; not friendly at all.

Hey champion - don't let the giants of criticism and slander defeat you. It's the Lord you're living for and He's rooting you on to victory!

GO FOR IT!

Eph 4:29-32 *(amp), "Let no foul or polluting language, nor evil word nor unwholesome or worthless talk (ever)come out of your mouth, but only such (speech) as is good and beneficial to the spiritual progress of others, as is fitting to the need and the occasion, that it may be a blessing and give grace (God's favor) to those who hear it.*

Denny's Alligator

My friend Denny Mullins was somewhat of a legend in the Dallas/Ft. Worth, Texas area. He was a big man - 6 foot 5", weighing around 270 or 280, and not fat. He played quarterback in college and could throw a football out of sight. Some people called him Bear Man because he wrestled bears (real bears). Denny was strong - very strong. One time he lifted up a one-horse trailer while his buddy changed the tire. (They didn't have a jack.)

Denny was unique in several ways. For instance - he didn't seem to be afraid of anything. He would get in a cage with a bear and appeared to be having a good time. He would come over to my house and flank and tie calves. Denny loved calf roping with all his heart! He could flank a small cow. He told me one time that he discovered that bears have a flank like a calf. He would grab a bear and throw him like a calf. Pretty amazing! Try this at home and you could get clawed and eaten!

Here's a Bear Man story. Denny and his friend Larry were rodeoing in Louisiana and they fell on financial hard times. They walked from the rodeo grounds to the carnival discussing what to do for gas money to get to the next rodeo. The first thing they see at the carnival is a cage with a sign over it that says, "$100 Prize for anyone who can stay in the cage with the alligator for 3 minutes." Now you've got to know as far as Denny was concerned, this was like money falling from heaven. This was the late sixties or early seventies, and $100 was quite a bit of money.

So here's Denny crawling into the cage. This cage was only about 3 feet tall so Denny went from 6'5" to about 2'8" on his hands and knees. Suddenly the alligator turns away from him. He thinks this is good! Wrong! Wham, the gator backlashes Denny with his tail. It breaks his nose and sends blood rushing down his face like a river. His eyes were blurred, blood every-

Denny Mullins

where and 2 minutes 45 seconds were still left on the clock!

Now, for the normal guy it's time to get out of Dodge and the alligator pen. But, not for Bearman! I can't remember how much more the alligator maimed him, but I do know he collected the $100. Psalm 34:7 David says, "I sought the Lord and he heard me and delivered me from all my fears." Denny wasn't intimidated. He was after the prize!

Isn't there something really cool about fearlessness? Clint Eastwood rides into town and nothing or no one fazes him. He is fearless. When we see what fear does, then we can appreciate the lack of it. Fear brings dread and torment. Fear paralyzes people. It takes the joy and freedom out of life. It makes you a coward; it tries to steal your dignity. Job said, "that which I greatly feared came upon me."

Fear also attracts all kinds of low-life devils. It brings the worst out in everyone. It causes you to lose when God created you to win - to live, to be fearless, joyful, happy and victorious! Did you know that every word in the Bible is packed with power; heavenly power from Almighty God. In John 1:14 it says, "The Word became flesh and dwelt among us." God's Word is His son Jesus. Do you want to be fearless? Seek God in His Word like David did and you will become the giant killer he was.

Set yourself on the inside to know Him, serve Him, and do great exploits with Him. Mind if I call you Bearman? Good, you're after the prize - you're crawling into the cage (where your gator is); you're not in familiar territory (great opportunity to trust Him). You take a hard slap; you're stunned, eyes blurred; losing blood fast. What have you gotten yourself into?! Good thing you pre-purposed, pre-determined, pre-prayed, and pre-believed to win!

Fearlessness - it's what God has for His champions!

GO FOR IT!

I John 4:18 (amp), *"There is no fear in love (dread does not exist), but full-grown (complete, perfect) love turns fear out of doors and expels every trace of terror! For fear brings with it the thought of punishment, and so he who is afraid has not reached the full maturity of love (is not yet grown into love's complete perfection).*

Marriage Tips

It t was your typical rodeo cowboy and cowgirl meeting. I was at the Calgary Stampede rodeo in Calgary, Alberta. One night myself and two other cowboys headed for the Ranchman's Bar. It was pretty much the hot spot in those days. I hadn't been there long when I noticed an attractive young lady wearing white pants. (Don't ask me why I noticed the white pants.) I asked her to dance and later sat down at the table with her and her lady friends. We laughed, talked, danced and drank. Well, that was July 1977. We had both been through divorces. She had been married to a millionaire living the jet set, big bucks, partying lifestyle. She found out that world wasn't what it was cracked up to be. I was looking for more than the championship I had won in 1975.

Without knowing it, we began to search for God. Fifteen months later we knelt down in our apartment in Ft. Worth, Texas and asked Jesus into our hearts. Three months later we were married in Ellensburg, Washington, September 1978. And you might guess, we lived happily ever after, right? Wrong! Even though your spirit man is bound for heaven when you get saved, your soul (which consists of your mind, will and emotions) needs to be changed into thinking and responding like the new creation it has become. **Rom.12:2** (niv) *"Do not conform to the pattern of this world, but be transformed by the renewing of your mind. Then you will be able to test and approve what God's will is - His good, pleasing and perfect will."*

The first four or five years were vivid reminders that we were full of ourselves more than the love of God. Our saving grace was our individual love for Jesus. He was our rock. When storms hit our marriage, instead of running from God, we would run to Him. The Holy Spirit would help us get past the hurt and misunderstanding and we would be going forward again. Scripture says we are to work out our salvation with fear and trembling. Boy, does that ever apply to a marriage. In the course of two people living together and trying to work out life's challenges together, it's no wonder even Christian marriages fail more than half the time from: money pressures, raising children and working out differences in life issues.

How about this one! One of you make a comment that is inappropriate or misunderstood. At any rate, a verbal encounter follows. Rather than getting better, it gets worse. How did it go so far? Maybe the issue wasn't even that big a deal. A storm erupts! Jesus talked about storms. **Matthew 7:24** (asv), *"Therefore, everyone who hears these words of mine and puts them into practice is like a wise man who built his house on a rock: and the rain descended, and the winds blew, and beat upon that house; and it fell not: for it was founded upon the rock."* Sherry and I want to encourage you to build your marriage on the Rock of God's Word. Today, our marriage is stronger and we are more in love now than ever. Loving and serving Jesus is the center of our marriage. Here are a few tips that have worked for us that may work for you:

1. Never say or threaten the D-word (divorce)

2. Be big enough to say, "I'm sorry."

3. Remember the commitment you made to each other, not just your feelings.

4. Don't rob God. Give your tithe, your 10% as a couple, to God. This will bring blessings to your finances.

5. Men, treat your wives like a precious jewel, that's what she is.

6. Women, your husband is your champion. If you treat him like one, he will live up to it.

7. When you have a fight, you don't have to be right.

8. Men, quit trying to explain. Sometimes it's better to say no more, give it time and it will be fine.

9. You and your wife are a power team for God. Because the enemy hates it, you'll both have to fight for it!

10. Have eyes for your mate only!

11. Discuss significant financial spending beforehand!

12. Always communicate kindly and call your mate some-

thing nice, like "darling," "wonderful," "sweetheart," (a special name).

13. The Lord spoke this to the heart of my friend, "I want you to overcome life's difficulties with two things: Love, Laughter." Sounds like a recipe for a successful marriage, doesn't it?

14. When you say your marriage vows you are sealing the strongest relationship bond known to man. It's called covenant. Study the meaning of this word thoroughly.

15. Never bring up the past. It's over.

Champion, if you will let Jesus mold and shape you into the man or woman that He wants you to be, your marriage will grow stronger and stronger. The Lord's Prayer reads, "Your kingdom come. Your will be done on earth as it is in heaven." God literally wants your marriage to be heaven on earth.

GO FOR IT!

John 13:34 *(esv), "A new commandment I give to you that you love one another; just as I have loved you, you also are to love one another."*

I Cor. 13:4-8 *(amp), "Love endures long and is patient and kind; love never is envious nor boils over with jealousy, is not boastful or vainglorious, does not display itself haughtily."*

Study these scriptures to bring life to your marriage.

Jeff and Sherry

Go On With It!

A s a young boy I had the privilege of personally being around great cowboys in the 50's and early 60's. It was so great to watch my dad (Deb Copenhaver), Bill Linderman, Casey Tibbs, Jim Shoulders, Harry Tompkins and so many other legends from that time period. The bucking stock in that era was exceptional also. It's hard to even explain how exciting it was when one of these top hands would draw the almost impossible bull or bronc. You would be on pins and needles waiting for the chute gate to open. Then it happens – an explosive contest between man and animal! It's like the cartoon of Pecos Bill riding a tornado. An example of this was when my dad drew an incredible bronc at the Ellensburg Stampede rodeo in 1956. Her name was Miss Klamath. At that time she had never been ridden.

With all the greatest rides that I personally witnessed from the sidelines, I noticed something special that would happen. Cowboys that were watching the ride would begin to holler something encouraging. The phrase that I remember the most was "go on with it." Right when it looked like everything was completely out of control and impossible, shouts of "go on" or "go on with it" would ring louder and louder. You could see the rider actually feed on these words. Right when you knew he was going to be launched off like a rocket, something in another dimension took over. He would go one more jump and then another and then the whistle. WOW! A great ride!! As a spectator you felt like you were part of a miracle. It was something you remembered for a lifetime.

Have you ever noticed the closer you get to your dream, the greater the pressure is? My friend, Leon Clift loves to remind me of this principle: "when you squeeze a balloon, the greatest pressure comes right before it pops." Are you sliding down onto a tough situation (bull or bronc) in your life? Is your body being attacked with disease or some difficult abnormality? Have you lost your job or has your business failed? Maybe you've messed up big time and ended up in prison. Is your family in turmoil and it looks like there's no way to resolve it. You're pursuing your dream, but it looks like you don't have the finances, resources or even the ability you need to get there.

Have you come this far to fail,- NO! Regardless of which life category you fall under, right now I have a word for you – GO ON WITH IT! I'm not speaking this to you – I'm shouting it! GO ON, GO ON, GO ON WITH IT! Is everything blurry from the wild bull spinning and lunging violently? Are you tense, aching with the pain of hanging on? Everything in you is crying – give it up – let go – I can't stand the fury! Right when everything reaches a pinnacle of impossibility, a voice cries out – "Go on with it my child." It's your heavenly father - your biggest fan and best friend! He says, "Go on, keep hanging on and spurring on to victory."

Never Give Up Champion!

GO FOR IT!

Heb 12:1-3 *(nlt)*

**Deb on Miss Klamath
Ellensburg, Washington 1952**

The Rooster

t was one of the hottest days of the summer as Sherry and I were driving into Fort Worth, Texas. In front of us we could see that cars ahead were swerving around something in the road. There in the middle of one lane was a large rooster standing totally still. We managed to miss him, and as we continued to drive down the road, we said to each other, "We need to pray for that rooster!" Then I surprised myself as I said, "Sherry, we need to go back to the rooster."

We immediately turned around on Hwy 377, a four-lane road from Granbury to Ft. Worth – a very busy, major highway. It was hard to believe the rooster was still alive and standing.

Sherry parked on the side of the road, and I walked out to the rooster very carefully to avoid getting run over myself. Traffic was moving all around me, and I'm sure everyone was wondering what was going on as I walked up to him. At first I tried shooing him off the road, but he wouldn't budge an inch. Then, I noticed his comb was bloody and laying on the side of his face. At this point I realized that because of the blood, and maybe shock; he couldn't see. I reached down and picked him up with no resistance on his part. As I put him in the car and placed him on the floor, we realized he had either been hit, fallen off a chicken truck, or suffered some such major catastrophe.

Sherry said, "We've got to get him some water." So, we pulled into a convenience store and got him a cup of water. He wouldn't drink, but he seemed to be doing a little better in the air conditioning. The heat on the highway that day was at least 115 to 120 degrees. Then she added, "We need to find a veterinarian." I don't think I would have thought of that, but we pulled into the closest veterinary hospital. There a lady responded to our problem with "we don't do roosters." We weren't too impressed with the response, but got directions to the next vet.

By now, we had named our feathered friend "Tuffy." We carried Tuffy into the vet and told a kind lady the whole story. During our conversation the vet asked, "Did you lay hands on this rooster for healing?" That's when we knew our prayers had been answered for Tuffy. They took the rooster to the back, put him on antibiotics and began to clean him up. The vet told us, "If he lives, I've got a hen on my ranch that he can stay with." As we pulled away from the vet clinic, we could barely believe this whole rooster episode. We had things to do in Ft. Worth, but all of a sudden they didn't seem that important.

The picture we began to see was the predicament that Sherry and I were in when we met one another; we didn't know Jesus. Sherry had been married to a millionaire and had recently divorced. She was looking for more than what money and a jet set life-style could offer. I had just won a world championship in calf roping and was looking for more than the fulfillment of a personal dream.

Our worlds even at the top of the heap had left us without hope – empty on the inside – somehow knowing the true meaning of life was missing. Yet there we were, like two roosters, standing in the middle of life's busy highway waiting for a disastrous end. Then guess what?

Someone cared enough to stop and lift us up. Someone cared enough to tell us the best news we would ever have now and forever. They told us about Jesus!

Scripture says, "While we were yet sinners, Christ died for us." While we were "goners - roosters in the road" – Jesus came to all of us and picked us up. He wrapped his arms around us and covered us with His eternal security. Listen to the first verses of **Psalm 91;** "He who dwells in the secret place of the Most High shall abide under the shadow of the Almighty. I will say of the Lord, he is my refuge and my fortress; my God, in Him I will trust. Surely He shall deliver you from the snare of the fowler and from the perilous pestilence. He shall cover you with His feathers, and under His wings you shall take refuge."

"He's there for the asking!"

P.S. I don't know how long Tuffy lived; but I do know the vet took him home and put him with his hen.

Champions Need A Mentor

⟴

Two of the great ropers of our time, Roy Cooper and Joe Beaver, were raised by outstanding calf ropers. These dads mentored their boys. Both won their first world championships in the 18-19 age bracket. Without the mentoring of roping wisdom it would have taken them longer, and most surely, they would have accomplished much less.

What is a mentor? It is someone who has been there - not talking or teaching out of theory, but experience. A mentor cares for you enough to tell you the truth. A true mentor isn't concerned necessarily if you like the truth he tells you or not; he knows it takes hard truth sometimes to keep advancing.

Are you familiar with the story of the rich young ruler? Jesus looked into this young man's heart and saw his weakness; then He gave him a tough word. **Mark 10:21**, *"Go, sell all your possessions and give the money to the poor, and follow me."* The young man wouldn't do it, and he walked away from the greatest mentor that ever lived. Do you have the desire to be a true champion? If you do, you will dive into God's Word to be mentored. It is the wisdom of the universe. Pray and ask God for a champion to mentor you in your dream and in your spiritual walk. He'll send you one. Mentors help you get your thinking right, they help you get a winning plan for life, and help you stay on the path to victory.

In the 90's the Dallas Cowboys had one of the great coaches (mentors) of all time. When he left town, the winning pretty much stopped! When Tiger Woods was coached by Butch Harmon, he held four majors at one time. When Butch left - things slowed down - way down.

When I was about 20 years old I got up the courage to ask the great eight-time calf roping champion, Dean Oliver, a question: "What do you think about when you back into the box?" He gave me eight words- eight words that mentored me the rest of my career and helped me tremendously. They were: "Get a good start, take a good throw." These became my only two conscious thoughts as I backed into the box the rest of my career. True mentors have the ability to simplify things and make them do-able.

Key words from a mentor can launch you into the next level of success that God has for you. In the early years of Jimmie Cooper's career, he had the privilege of traveling with World Champion Tom Ferguson. Tom knew many of the intricate details of winning - how to enter, learning to read cattle, how to get out of the barrier - strategies for different rodeo situations. This led to an all-around world championship for Jimmie. Great mentors are easy to learn from, because they are teaching and training out of love to improve others and from their personal experience.

Pray and ask God to bring the mentor or mentors that He has for your life. He will do it - He loves you and wants you to win!

GO FOR IT!!

I Cor 4:15, (the message), "There are a lot of people around who can't wait to tell you what you've done wrong; but there aren't many fathers (mentors) willing to take the time and effort to help you."

Jeff at month long roping school in Granbury, Texas

God Still Speaks to His People

*I*t was the early 1980's and I was at one of my very favorite rodeos; Omak, Washington. Omak is one of the first class rodeos in the Northwest, and I was always excited to be there. I was praying one afternoon and the Lord began to speak to me in my heart. Now, this may sound out of the ordinary to you; it was for me too! The Lord said "you're going to draw calf #32." In my heart, I said back to HIM; I can tie this calf in 7 seconds. This calf was probably the best calf in rodeo history --he ran about 5 miles an hour and weighed about 170 lbs.

When I said, in my heart,"I can tie him in 7 seconds," the Lord said –"something is going to happen and you're going to be a short eight." Well, two hours later, I went up to the roping chute and the judges were drawing the calves out of about a 40-calf herd. When they got to my name, the judge reached into the hat and pulled out a poker chip with a number on it and said, "Jeff Copenhaver – 32!" Wow! I got excited – the first part of what the Lord showed me came true. Calf #32 ran so slow that I shortened my rope about 4 feet which I had never done before. As I backed into the box to compete, I was excited to have a great calf; but even more so that the Lord was confirming what HE had spoken in my heart.

Omak was a fairly long score which means the calf is given a fairly long head start. Yet this calf was so slow I still roped him in 2 swings. I was down the rope and flanked him faster than any run in my life. As I flanked him though, something went crazy. The calf was pulled out of my hands and went about 8 feet toward my horse. As I looked up at my horse, I saw what had happened. My jerk line wrapped around my horse's front legs; he was scared and running backwards. He must have thought it was a snake or something! When he quit dragging the calf I could finally tie him. After all the trouble I had I was still only 8.2 seconds, which still set a new arena record.

Now, remember my dialogue with the Lord in prayer – HE said "you're going to draw calf #32." I said, "I can tie him in 7 seconds." HE said, "Something is going to happen and you will be a short eight." You can see who got the last word. To me what is so incredible is that God knows everything and HE knows the end from the beginning. He knew exactly what calf I would draw and exactly what would happen before it happened. Is God real? Does HE still speak to HIS people? Does HE know your future and does HE care? Yes, yes, yes, yes!

Now, He may not always speak as clearly to us as He happened to speak to me that day; but He does speak to us more often than we realize and in many different ways. Pray and listen for that still small voice.

He still speaks to His people today!

Isaiah 30:21 *niv, "Whether you turn to the right or to the left, your ears will hear a voice behind you saying, "This is the way; walk in it."*

John 10:27 *My sheep hear my voice, and I know them, and they follow me.*

Jeff on Sugar NFR 1978

Really Hungry

By Sherry Copenhaver

Have you ever been hungry? I mean really, really, really hungry? Most everyone has felt that way at one time or another. Thank God that we are living in a country where famine, prolonged hunger, and starvation are not a predominant concern as in most third world countries. The majority of us have the privilege of eating out at a restaurant or sitting down to a wonderful meal prepared by our mother or wife. When you do, you savor every bit, each morsel and devour everything until it is gone.

That happened to me not long ago after we had been fasting and seeking the Lord for a period of time; then we got to eat again. I had my favorite meal at Luby's Cafeteria in Ft. Worth. They have an out-of-this-world almond-crusted baked fish. I coupled it up with candied sweet potatoes and yummy green beans with bacon, topped off with key lime pie. It was worth waiting for – I can still taste it! This meal was so completely satisfying, and I was so wonderfully happy that my stomach was full. Then, guess what? – not really to my surprise - but about six hours later, the hunger cycle began to repeat itself, and I was hungry again. Amazing how that works!

God is kinda' like that in our everyday life with Him. Daily He desires to interact with us, and daily we should be hungering and thirsting after Him. **Luke 6:21** says, *"Blessed are you who hunger now, for you shall be filled."* Also, **Psalm 34:8** says, *"Oh, taste and see that the Lord is good."* Taste buds are a powerful part of our body. For example: if you have grown up on sugar, cereal, soft drinks, and lots of desserts; chances are you have a sweet tooth and a big taste for sugar. If you weren't allowed much candy, soda pop, or sugar as a child (much like the Australian people, who are very healthy), you probably have not acquired a great taste for sweets.

That's the way it is in the spiritual world concerning kingdom principles from God's Word. I'm referring to living as a

Christian with Jesus Christ as your Lord. It's normal and spiritually healthy for you to be hungry for the things of God; to read His Word daily, and to have a private and personal time with Him daily. You'll be drawing on His strength and life-giving spirit, wanting to attend church faithfully and be a part of God's family – rather than dreading the thought of church on Sunday, and making excuses to stay away.

It should be normal for you to desire to associate with Christian friends or acquaintances as your buddies – to hang out with them, rather than individuals that influence your life in the wrong way. The apostle Paul asked, "What communion has light with darkness?" **1 John 1:5** tells us, *"God is light and in Him is no darkness at all."* Actually, it should be normal to pack your Bible everywhere you go, unashamedly on your truck dash, in your car, on your office desk, etc. Read it daily – every day of your life!

You eat every day, don't you? Well, God's Word is your vital necessity – your daily bread (**John 6:35**), your protection against the enemy (**Psalm 91**), and your counsel and guide (**Proverbs 2**). Oh, the benefits of eating good food daily for your body – it keeps you alive and healthy. It's the same with the Word of God that feeds your spirit man and keeps him strong. Can you imagine if you didn't feed your body for days, weeks, and months? You'd be weak, wimpy, malnourished, sickly and finally – dead! Regretfully, that's how some Christians look to God. Remember, the Bible says in **I Thessalonians 5:23**, *"You are a spirit, you live in a body and you have a soul (mind, will, and emotions)."* You serve a spiritual God. Just because you can't see Him doesn't mean He's not real or not there. He's more real than the air that you breathe!

God sees us through spiritual eyes and discerns and knows all of our hearts. He longs for those who seek Him to ask Him questions. Research His Word, don't just read it. Look up words in the dictionary to gain a broader understanding. It's time to seek God and understand that we are spiritual beings living in a spiritual kingdom. .if, indeed, you believe you are a new creation in Christ (**II Corinthians 5:17**), walking in new spiritual laws and principles.

In actuality, we are just passing through this physical world for a season, in preparation for eternity in heaven. So, get hungry for God. Make yourself hungry! Don't sit around waiting for God to do it. Acquire a taste for Him – pray for it with all your heart. The Bible says a man's strong spirit will sustain him in the day of trouble (**Proverbs 18:14**). How do you expect to overcome and triumph through trials if you have a weak, sickly spirit with little strength to draw upon when encountering a test?

Being hungry for God is natural and healthy and will keep you from being a weak, wimpy, barely-saved Christian. In the morning, serve yourself a big helping of God's Word; it's the breakfast of Champions! Jesus is Lord!

Sherry competing in English Pleasure on her horse Cody in 1972.

Christianity Is Givianity

I was going to Kansas City in November 1979 with my good friend Nolan Lewallen. We were both brand new Christians and were excited about our walk with God. We mutually agreed to going on a three day fast, no food for three days.

After wondering if we were going to starve, we found out when you seek Him in fasting and prayer, good things happen. At the end of the fast the Lord spoke in my heart – "Christianity is givianity and giving is love in action." For the first time in my life I realized what life was all about. As I was riding my horse in their small exercise arena, a lady in the crowd next to the arena grabbed her heart and collapsed on the concrete. Before I could give it a conscious thought, I jumped off my horse over the fence to pray for this lady. Within a few minutes the lady was up and fine.

There's no doubt in my mind why I jumped that fence so suddenly; I realized why God created me: To love Him and love others! The Lord has called us all to do the same. The Lord spoke to my wife, Sherry, in the same time period and gave her a similar message. He spoke in her heart, "If you'll reach out to meet the needs of others, I'll see to it that your needs are met!"

About that same time, the Lord gave me a vision or picture of what my life had been all about. I was standing inside a circle of hundreds of business card-sized mirrors. Every little mirror was me, (or about me) my horse, my truck, my dreams, my desires, it was all me, me, me. Now get this: when I would read the Word of God and do what it said to do – the Holy Spirit would take this tiny hammer and tap, tap, tap on one of these mirrors. The mirror would break then be replaced by a window. As I looked through the window, I could see others – their wants, their needs, and their desires.

My whole approach to life changed. I realized that God put me on the earth to reach out, help and be a blessing to others. Kids that I used to ignore at rodeos, I would talk to and sign autographs for. I wanted to encourage them, and help them know and live for the Lord.

In the eighties, a steer wrestler named Cliff Armstrong would wear a superman shirt underneath his cowboy shirt. Get this: When he would throw a super fast steer, Cliff would run toward the grandstand, rip open his cowboy shirt and there would be the super "S." The crowd would go absolutely crazy! **Hebrews 12:1** (Living Bible) reads, *"Since we have such a huge crowd of men of faith watching us from the grandstands, let us strip off anything that slows us down or holds us back, and especially those sins that wrap themselves so tightly around our feet and trip us up: and let us run with patience the particular race that God has set before us."*

There you go – a grandstand of faith cheering us on. If you know Jesus and are willing to let Him break the mirrors and reveal the windows, then you are wearing the super "S" shirt! Jesus has a super life for you. You have His ability and His power living in you. The power to win comes from within! It's the higher life He told us about in John 10:10, (amp), "The thief comes only in order to steal and kill and destroy. I came that they may have life and enjoy life, and have it in abundance (to the full, till it overflows).

Christianity is Givianity, Champion

Go For It!

Spud Tindell, David Young, Dave Burrows, and Darryl Baker at the 30th Cowboy Church Anniversary

Match Roping In Cuba

It was 1998 and eight of us - my wife, daughter, and 5 other cowboys were on our way to Cuba. Where? Our friend Richard Ashley from Mexico, who was our interpreter, had set it up to go there and teach calf roping. Cuba was having its annual finals rodeo that included rodeo teams competing from Central America, South America and Mexico. It was a big deal; and we were excited to be there. Our guys competed at the event and then we taught rodeo clinics during the day. One of our guys, Jack Stephenson, was there to introduce the sport of team roping in Cuba. Eugene Weldon was our steer wrestling coach. Our clinic was in Havana at their big rodeo fair grounds.

The last night we were there was a big celebration on the top floor of the Havana Hilton. We were blessed that the Cuban officials had us stand up to thank us for coming and helping improve the skill level of Cuban rodeo. After our school at Havana we got the news that the Cuban cowboys in the town of Sancti Spiritus didn't know if they were interested in Americans coaching them. Consequently they set up a match roping between their champion calf roper and our guy - Matt Keil. The unsaid message was that if the Cubans won, we could take our school on down the road.

We get to Sancti Spiritus and their arena is full of people excited to watch a U.S - Cuban match roping. It didn't take a rocket scientist to figure out who they were rooting for either! Now here's the problem - a huge one! The horse we borrow is a nice horse but the saddle on him is about a 1930's model. That means that the stirrup leathers are the old time lace up version. Today's saddles have quick change stirrups. The owner of our

Cuban calf horse is 6 ft 4 in. tall - Matt is 5'7" or 5'8". There was no way that Matt could stand up in his stirrups to rope a calf.

Guess what? It's time to pray and cowboy up. In that order. The Cuban champion roped first and he was around 12 to 13 seconds. Matt's up - he rides after his calf and tries to touch his stirrups on tippy toes. As could be expected his loop hits the calf on the back of the neck - a miss. No, wait! The rope bounces off his back and goes around his neck! Glory to God - divine intervention! He ties the calf in about the same time as his competitor. Thank you Lord! Game on! Our competitor, Nicolas, ties his next calf in the long 11 second range. Here goes Matt again. He runs up to his calf - not able to stand up in his stirrups - he's sitting flat

Roping school Havana, Cuba

Matt match roping Sanctus Spiritus, Cuba

Roping school, Sanctus Spiritus, Cuba

in the saddle. If you are a tie down calf roper or a breakaway roper, you know that this isn't going to work.

The second run was identical to the first. Sitting flat in the saddle, he throws his rope and hits the calf between the back of his head and shoulders. At this point all I can tell you is there is a God in Israel! For the second time the rope ricocheted off his back and went around his neck. True story - I witnessed it yet I could barely believe it! Matt was 10.7 seconds. He was leading after 2 calves. The Cuban champion roped his final calf in the 12 second range. Good news for him - he had them all roped and tied down.

Pressure on! The potential success of our whole trip comes down to this last calf! I walked up to Matt before he ran his third and last calf and told him, "You might try roping this one." He said, "You noticed, did you?" Here's the good news - he actually roped his third calf (around the neck) and tied the calf in 8.5 seconds - probably the fasted calf ever tied in Cuba at that time. It was like Rocky IV and the crowd went wild cheering for Matt.

Because we won, the next day we had our roping school in Sancti de Spiritus. While I was coaching,, my wife Sherry and our interpreter Richard Ashley got to lead the Cuban champion and his wife to the Lord!

I love this story - for this reason. Many people don't realize that God can and will use their gifts and talents - to fulfill His purposes. Matt had no idea that his ability to rope would make all the difference in the success of our trip. It proves that all that God needs is our availability. Are you a farmer, rancher, doctor, student, lawyer, hunter or business man? None of that matters. If your heart is to glorify God and be used of Him; get ready! You may find yourself like Matt - in another country; in a showdown with everything on the line. Are you saying I don't have to be Billy Graham for Jesus to use me? That's right, just bring whatever you have to the King. He will take it and use it for His glory!.

GO FOR IT!

I Cor. 1:4 *(nlt)*, *"I always thank my God for you and for the gracious gifts he has given you, now that you belong to Christ Jesus.*

Prov. 18:16 *(amp)*, *A man's gift makes room for him and brings him before great men.*

The "IT" is "ER"

⚬⚬⚬

A few years ago I was teaching a calf roping school in Billings, Montana. My friend Spud Tindell was leaving the school and he told the kids, "If you ever find out what the IT in GO FOR IT! is, then Go For it!" He was referring to my favorite saying. I've written three GOD WANTS YOU TO WIN devotionals and at the end of most of the articles, I write GO FOR IT!

Now get this, I'm teaching another roping school this time in Kansas and God speaks to my heart saying, "The IT is ER!" What? I said in my heart. Again He spoke in my heart the IT in GO FOR IT is ER. I told a friend of mine about this and he said "ER" is a Hebrew word. I looked up ER in the Hebrew Strong's Concordance and ER means "wake up or stir up." Here I am at this school encouraging my guys to work harder, go faster, be wiser, and rope sharper. Everything was ER, ER, ER, and ER. The IT is ER! You wanna GO FOR IT? Well, the IT is ER! I want to stir you up, wake you up and open your eyes to the greatness that God has for your life. You are His special champion. He loves you so much! Now, get in faith - lock on to believing Him! Become a dream-er. Hook up with God and let Him make you tend-er, kind-er, nic-er and clos-er to Him. He will make things plain-er, clear-er, bright-er; He will make you tough-er, strong-er and cause you to go farther.!

As I'm writing this, I can see David running toward Goliath with his sling shot. He was going for it! I shared what the Lord showed me with my students and guess what? We got it! That night we stayed longer. We went faster, we roped wiser, and we strategized to get stronger. God wants us to face our giants and enter into the promised land that He has ordained and planned for us from the foundation of the world." Go For It" means let's see what you've got! You're facing a giant - but guess what? God is on your side champion!

The Apostle Paul said in **Phil 3:14** ,"*This one thing I do, forgetting the things which are behind and reaching forth into those things* which are before; I press toward the mark for the prize of the high calling of God in Christ Jesus." The ER wakes us up and stirs us up to press toward the prize that God has for us!. Champions don't settle for less! They aren't passive, they aren't content with mediocrity. It's time to saddle up your faith horse and ride faster. Are you a worker, a laborer, in God's kingdom? The Bible says you are an overcom-er!

Yes sir! the "IT" is "ER"!

GO FOR IT!

Eccl. 9:10 (niv), "Whatever your hand finds to do, do it with all your might. . .."

The "IT" is "ER".

A Champion Who Gave His All

I recently received this letter from Alabama:

"Jeff,

I bought an old sorrel horse from you about six years ago after attending your week-long school. Jody and I came to get the horse in September of that year. If you remember Old Sorrely, he wouldn't win a halter class, but his heart was as big as Texas. No matter where I hauled that horse, I almost always got comments about his hustle. In our little practice pen, people talked about him like he was a world champion – because he gave 110% every time you backed him in the box.

After I had him 2 or 3 years, I could tell he was losing a step or two, so I let a local high school rodeo kid ride him in breakaway for a season. She missed going to the finals, but got a scholarship to Fort Scott Community College, and won over $2000 at local amateur rodeos in the summer before she started school. Old Sorrely did OK in Kansas, but the second year at Fort Scott, she bought another horse and I got Sorrely back and retired him. This past summer he has been baby sitting a foal while I weaned her. He is down much of the time and has great difficulty walking.

I am writing to tell you that I am putting Sorrelly to sleep this morning and burying him in my back pasture. While I haven't used this horse for two years, my wife reminded me last night how much I am going to miss him. I don't know whether Sorrelly came my way to teach me to calf rope, to teach lessons about "trying" to the local cowboys, or to win a college scholarship for that young lady, but I appreciate you for hooking me up with him. He is a friend I will always remember.

Dan Henry

Isn't it amazing – all the lives who were watching this little sorrel horse; and who were touched by his life? Whether you realize it or not, people are watching you – at school, on your job, in your community, or wherever you happen to be. You are an example, a witness, and a role model in your world. The good character qualities that reside in your life are a comfort, an inspiration, and a source of strength in the lives of others. Keep pressing forward– people are watching – your life is making a difference!

GO FOR IT!!

Sorrelly in action

Champions Wait for the Victory

⬥⟩⟩⟩⟩⟩⬥

The year was 1971 and I had a dream in my heart. I had never been to a national finals rodeo, but I was now in pursuit. I had a good horse who was working real good and I felt that I was roping pretty good; but by now after not placing in 9 rodeos in a row I was questioning that.

I was roping at the Salt Palace in Salt Lake City and I had roped a calf fairly quick and then guess what? My right stirrup falls off and darts me into the ground like a scud missile - 10 rodeos in a row - no money! I knew I had to find a "duck off" rodeo (that would be easier than the average rodeo.) I entered a little rodeo in Montana that had 12 ropers - well, I won second! Can you believe it? It paid a gigantic $120. But guess what? I had a check with my name on it! The Red Sea had split!

You can't believe what that second place did on the inside of me. Little did I know that this would spark a turnaround that would send me to my first NFR. I went to Newport, Washington - a two header and won first. Then I won Omak, WA; Moses Lake, WA; Kalispell, MT; Bremerton, WA; Kennewick, WA; La Grande, OR; Walla Walla, WA; and Lewiston, ID - all first places. Then I won a go round at Pendleton, OR and first place at Puyallup, WA. From losing at ten rodeos to winning ten rodeos. I couldn't sleep the night before I roped because I knew I was going to win. I knew I would draw a good calf - I knew things were going to go right. I knew I could do it.

When we read and study our Bibles we see countless examples of extreme turnarounds. Abraham, Joseph, Noah, Joshua, Caleb, Ruth, Esther, and the list goes on and on. Men and women of God, who put their trust in the awesome, glorious, victorious God.

Read this scripture: Psalm 34:19, "Many are the afflictions of the righteous. But the Lord delivers him out of them all."

When you get hooked up with Jesus Christ and begin to read His Word, you realize He wants you to win. He can turn losing into winning in the snap of a finger - dreams spoiled into dreams realized. Here we go, now! You've spent the time in preparation. The stage is set. You believe you can do it. You've had a season of losing, that's over now! Trust in the One who lives in you and be confident in the "one He lives in." Ten losses - ten wins. It's time for a turnaround champion!

GOD WANTS YOU TO WIN!

GO FOR IT!

Prov. 25:15, *(living Bible),"Be patient and you will finally win."*

Jeff at Houston Astrodome 1971

The Bible Challenge

$\sim\!\!\infty\!\!\sim$

Expect the best, prepare for the worst.

My friend Scott Mendes called me one night and presented me with an unusual offer. Scott is a former World Champion bull rider who is also a committed Christian. Because of his connections in his ministry with the television industry, he was asked to put a team together to compete in the "American Bible Challenge" which is a national TV program hosted by Jeff Foxworthy. He was looking for two more Christian cowboys to make a three-man team. When we were interviewed in Dallas; we were given a Bible-question test. I had the highest score on our team, so I was appointed captain. I was excited about it because I had been a Bible enthusiast since I was saved in 1978. Scott invited his bull rider friend Kelly Clark to be the third member of the team. Kelly has taught Bible study in his church for years. Scott had pastored for some time and has always loved God's word. Our team was called the Cowboy Crusaders. YEE HAW!

We were pumped! We prepared and studied every possible Bible story, scripture and Bible character that we could possible imagine. We would spend hours testing each other. We bought Bible games and went through hundreds of Bible question cards. After about three weeks of this, I found myself unable to sleep because I had literally hundreds of Bible facts and scriptures cross-firing through my brain. Whether this contest had stirred up a "competitive spirit" in us or just the hope of winning money for Scott's ministry; either way we were ready.

We flew into Los Angeles the night before and the next day we were being schooled on how the game works - what to do and what not to do. Here we go! Game on! The first part of the game was more like a picnic game (which we hadn't prepared for). We didn't do so well. In the next phase, we each had a buzzer in front of us. They were fairly easy questions so with three teams and nine players everyone hit their buzzers simultaneously. The only problem was I don't think ours worked.

Whatever! So then they began to ask questions that were partially based on knowledge of children's games. OK - moving on - as team captain I was given the last question. In my opinion it was kind of a trick question. I missed it! Strike three - the Crusaders were out! And I do mean out - before we had barely begun it was over!

As we walked behind the set, I can't describe the feelings I had. It was a combination of extreme disappointment, frustration, shame, embarrassment, regret with a little bit of anger thrown in there too. I had questions. Was this fair? Was this right? Is this happening for real or is it a bad dream that I will wake up from? My disappointment wasn't about the money or even the competition. Our team wanted to show America that there are men who love God's Word and are committed and excited about the things of God. We wanted to be an example and encouragement to the younger generation . Time has passed since we returned home from Hollywood. Time helps!

I've been a Dallas Cowboy fan for a long time. We used to have church super bowl parties in the 90's when the Cowboys were winning super bowl rings. Well, recently the Cowboys were on the playoff trail - looking really good. At a critical time late in the game they threw a touchdown pass that was incredible - off the graph! Then to the shock of everyone, a challenge flag was thrown. To the shock of Dallas fans the touchdown was erased. They said it was not a legal catch. What? The hopes for a championship obliterated. Is this right? Can this be happening for real? Maybe it's just a bad dream that we can wake up from! Wow! Feelings of disappointment, frustration, anger, etc. were the norm.

Is there an incident in your life that has been flashing like a billboard in your mind? Maybe you've messed up big time! It might have been the biggest opportunity in your life and you blew it. Or perhaps someone else did wrong and you got the blame for it! At any rate you're having a hard time going forward. Divorce, bankruptcy, jail, or public embarrassment may be involved - the potential negative life - scenarios are endless. Is there a way to learn and even improve our quality of life when we confront some of these difficult storms?

These tips could be beneficial to you:

1. Find someone (they are everywhere) who is going through similar challenges as you've had or are having. Then pray for them, encourage them and help them overcome. Sow

the seed of love into other's dreams and challenges and watch God help yours.

2. Be thankful! Yeah, you lost and it hurt! But you can be thankful that today is a new day. I believe your chance to win will come again! The Apostle Paul said, "This one thing I do. Forgetting the past and looking forward to what lies ahead, I press on to reach the end of the race and receive the heavenly prize for which God through Christ Jesus, is calling us."

3. Never let a negative, tough situation define your life or hinder your progress. Instead, let it propel and ignite you to do better than ever! Question: what defines who you are? Is it how many victories you are able to accumulate in your lifetime. Is it how perfectly you perform in your moments of opportunity? Or is it your resolve to go on, to get back up, to leave that moment of hurt and pain and purpose in your faith (and heart of hearts) to see a better day. I believe that God wants us to look to Him and what His word says. Extreme disappointment can define you and potentially destroy you; or spur you on to greater dedication and determination to win!

Hey champion, which will it be for you?

1 Peter 5:6-7 *says, " We should humble ourselves under God's mighty hand! How? By casting the whole of your care (all your anxieties, all your worries, all your con-cerns) once and for all on Him for He cares for you affectionately and cares about you watchfully. "*

Champions Go "Hay Hoppin"

———❦❦❦———

H ave you ever flown in a small airplane in hot or rough weather? If you have, you probably know what it's like to get real sick up there in the air! Well, the true story goes that my Dad and another legendary bronc rider Casey Tibbs were working the two Labor Day rodeos in Walla Walla and Ellensburg, Washington. They were in Walla Walla in the hotel lobby when Larry Daniels (a bull rider-pilot) asked Dad and Casey if they wanted to catch a ride in his plane to Ellensburg. They said "sure," so away they went.

Dad was in the front with Larry and there was another bull rider in the back seat with Casey. Well, everything was somewhat normal until they got into the Yakima valley south of Ellensburg. This is big hay country; and there were stacks of square bales in the fields. Now, don't ask me if this was Larry's everyday sense of perverted humor or if he secretly hated his flying companions. Perhaps he was a Kamikaze wanna-be. He said, "have you guys ever been hay hoppin?" I'm sure no one answered. Larry gasses the plane toward the closest hay stack – flying about 2 feet above the ground, and just barely before he hits it, he shoots for the sky. A near miss! Then off to the next stack. Same thing! I don't know for sure how many "hay hoppin" stacks he jumped but after the 3rd stack Casey threw up big time all over Dad in the front seat. The bull rider in the back seat got deathly sick and instead of throwing up, he had a major accident in his pants. The life of cowboys in that era was never boring.

Now, no one has any luggage; all their clothes are back in Walla Walla - not really a setting for a Wrangler commercial. Well, they fly on to the Ellensburg airport and found the perfect answer to their predicament - a fire hose. Dad takes his shirt off and the bull rider takes his pants off and they turned the fire hose on both of them. Then while they're still wet, they put them back on.

The rest of the story is that Dad had drawn a horse named Export; and the bull rider has a bull named Ought, as in zero. Ought had never been ridden up to that time, and was close to impossible to ride. Well, Dad wins the go round on Export and our (dried-out jeans) partner rides Ought, making one of the greatest rides Dad had ever seen.

Have you ever seen the Clint Eastwood movie Heartbreak Ridge? Clint's a marine drill sergeant that is making marine men out of older boys. His favorite saying was "improvise and overcome." Regardless of what they encountered, it was improvise and overcome! How about these cowboys encountering some difficulties – some real life messes; then improvising and overcoming and seeing great victory!

Sometimes dealing with big life messes makes us more mature, and more caring for what others are going through. Plus we don't take ourselves so seriously. What are you going through today? Is it a divorce, bankruptcy, losing a loved one, sickness, prison, devastating effects of drugs or alcohol? Maybe you've lost your children because you were an unfit mother or father. Are you going through something really embarrassing or humiliating?

Instead of inviting guilt and shame to rule in your life, do like these guys. Let God bring the water hose of His Word into your life and wash away the mess! Now, guess what –

IT'S TIME FOR YOUR VICTORIOUS RIDE
YOUR GREATEST VICTORY!
GO FOR IT!

I John 5:4 *(niv),* *"for everyone born of God overcomes the world. This is the victory that has overcome the world, even our faith."*

Fuzzy Calf

～∞∞∞～

I was in Regina, Saskatchewan in November 1989. Now if you want to visit Regina, my advice is not to go there in November. One year it was 38 degrees below zero. I was excited though, because I was competing at their rodeo which was the first big pro-rodeo that counted for the next years standings. It was unique for me because it was the first time that I had worn my shirt that had a big J.E.S.U.S. on the sleeve. I backed into the box that night and as I got ready to nod my head, I remember thinking to myself: "this calf is really fuzzy!" My vision was so poor that all I could see was this fuzzy animal in front of me. I roped that night (obviously by the grace of God), and tied my calf in 9.3 seconds. I won the rodeo, which was the good news. The bad news was that I needed better vision, big time!

I can remember praying and asking God for help! Then I went to an optometrist in Ft. Worth, Texas who fitted me in glasses. The glasses didn't really help. Then I went back to him and he fitted me in soft contact lenses. They didn't help either, so he had me wear soft contacts and glasses together. Still, no good!

Then a friend of mine told me, "you should go see these two optometrists that just moved to Granbury." Well, here's the rest of the story. I go to the Cook brothers. They diagnose my eyes with a condition called keratoconus (an eye condition that 1 out of 15,000 people have.) The Cook brothers were pioneers in keratoconus lenses. They had been part of developing special lenses that would give people vision with this eye condition. They moved to what town? My town! Two of the very few people on the planet that could recognize my condition and actually help me!

Do you see what happened? I prayed. God heard my prayer and answered it in a magnificent, amazing way - like only He can! **Jeremiah 32:27** says, *"Is there anything too hard for me, says the Lord?"* This is the third devotional I've written, and I want you to know that a recurring message seems to be surfacing. It's not intentional, but it keeps flowing out of my life stories since I've become a Christian. God loves you! He wants you to come to Him in prayer; He will go to great lengths to answer those prayers.

What challenges, difficulties or impossibilities exist in your life? Is there something 'fuzzy" in your life that only God can make clear? Jesus loves you and there's nothing that He can't or won't do for you! The end of your strength and ability can be the beginning of His - if you'll pray and believe Him!

GO FOR IT!!!

Hebrews 4:16 *(amp), "Let us then fearlessly and confidently and boldly draw near to the throne of grace (the throne of God's unmerited favor to us sinners), that we may receive mercy (for our failures) and find grace to help in good time for every need (appropriate help and well-timed help, coming just when we need it).*

I John 5:14-15 *(KJV), "And this is the confidence that we have in him, that, if we ask any thing according to his will, he hears us: And if we know that he hears us, whatsoever we ask, we know that we have the petitions that we desired of him."*

Fuzzy Calf

Champions Know They Need The Best Equipment

G rowing up I can remember the first saddle I ever owned. My Dad bought my sister Debbie and me the coolest kid saddles. To have my own personal saddle was bigger than life itself! Years later I got to ride Dad's 1955 Madison Square Garden saddle - he won New York two times, and I was always eyeing those saddles. In the early 70's, somehow I talked Dad out of his 1955 World Championship saddle. It was a Rowell saddle made in Hayward, California, and it was the best of the best. I cannot describe the feeling I had riding that saddle; not only was it an incredible saddle, but it was a champion's saddle. I felt like a champion when I got on it. Did you know that God wants you to be equipped with the best of the best?

One day the Lord dropped in my heart that if salvation (being born again) is the horse, (being filled or baptized with the Holy Spirit) is the saddle. Now, I don't know about you but I wouldn't attempt anything fancy on a horse riding bareback. A good saddle is a comfort and a wonderful help to complete a winning ride.

Did you know that God has a supernatural prayer language for you? God has a heavenly hot line - kind of like the President's hot line to the Pentagon. Sherry and I received Jesus in June 1978; a month later we were baptized in water in the swimming pool at Little America (Cheyenne, Wyoming). Then the next day we were baptized or filled with the Holy Spirit. Next to receiving Jesus, it's the greatest thing that has ever hap-

pened to us. That night in July 1978, a calf roper's wife prayed with Sherry and me to receive the baptism of the Holy Spirit. Some people call it the infilling of the Holy Spirit. No matter what you call it, it is Bible and it is wonderful! (**Acts 1:8, Acts 19:1-6, Acts 8:14-17**) **Luke 11:13** (nlt), *"So if you sinful people know how to give good gifts to your children, how much more will your heavenly Father give the Holy Spirit to those who ask him."*

Four dynamic things happened almost immediately. #1 we went back to our motel room, and we were incredibly convicted that we were not to have sexual relations anymore outside of marriage (We were not married at the time). Now, it's important to clarify something here, we already knew in scripture this was sin, but it was the power of the Holy Spirit that caused us to repent (or stop). #2 We had an incredible desire to read and study (literally eat) God' s word. (**Matt.4:4**) We sat under a pine tree close to the entrance of Cheyenne's Frontier Park and read an amplified version Bible. The desire to hear from God through His word was absolutely amazing. #3 For the first time Sherry and I began to pray out loud together. Before the Holy Spirit's power, that was almost unheard of. We were no longer intimidated. What an awesome helper. What an incredible "saddle." #4 We got a supernatural prayer language. I was so absolutely amazed because I had tried to learn Latin in Junior High and nearly flunked. It was so hard. Now, overnight I could speak another language - a heavenly one!

For years as a calf roping coach, when someone asked me what kind of saddle to buy I would tell them a handful of the outstanding custom saddle makers in the country. Their response usually was "I can't afford that" - my response is ,"you can't afford (for the sake of you and your horse) anything less than the best."

Christian, God wants you to be equipped with the best of the best.

CHAMPION - THE PERSON OF THE HOLY SPIRIT WANTS TO TAKE YOU ON A VICTORIOUS RIDE!

John 16:7 *(amp), "However, I am telling you nothing but the truth when I say it is profitable (good, expedient, advantageous) for you that I go away. Because if I do not go away, the Comforter (Counselor, Helper, Advocate, Intercessor, Strengthener, Standby) will not come to you {into close fellowship with you}; but if I go away, I will send Him to you [to be in close fellowship with you.]*

The Impossi-Bull

———∞∞∞———

Many years ago at the National Finals Rodeo in Oklahoma City, Freckles Brown rode the famous bull Tornado. He was unridden at the time, totally awesome. On top of Tornado looking unrideable, Freckles was in his forties, by the world's standard, past the age of even attempting such a feat. Well, that night Freckles had faith that the "almost impossible was possible." It was a night for rodeo history.

I believe God has placed in every human being on the planet the desire to do the impossible. However, many people - because of fear, doubt, unbelief, and countless other things - will never step into that life. When we are born again by the Spirit of God, we have the nature of God actually living in us. **Luke 1:37**, *"With God all things are possible."* Well, there you go. He's in us. He's for us, and He's working with us and through us.

We built a log church in Granbury, Texas, from 1994 to 1997. Many said we would never finish it - too big an undertaking. Well, we kept walking and working by faith (believing Jesus), and in October of 1997 it was completed. What has God put in your heart, champion, that people would tell you can't be done? Or maybe the battle is in your mind and all those negative thoughts cry out to you "this is crazy, you better not even dream of doing this, let alone start taking actual steps to get it done."

"Remember: He - not thee--split the Red Sea." He created the entire universe and manufactured you. He's the potter, you're the clay. He made everything and can do anything - especially the impossible. In the light of all this, what are you waiting for? Why wouldn't you launch out? Put all your disappointments and failures of the past behind you.

Now, go on a journey with me. I want you to picture your dream - that thing that God has placed in your heart that seems so incredibly impossible. Only on this journey, that thing becomes Tornado. See yourself looking into the chute with respect for a bull that's never been ridden. Yes, that's right - never! You climb up the chute with your bull rope and begin to put it on him, wondering what went through the minds of those who tried before you. Were they honestly hopeful to achieve the impossible, or almost paralyzed with fear?

At any rate, it's not them, now, it's you. You are up now and as the announcer is calling your name and Tornado's, you slide your hand into the handle of your rope. As someone pulls your rope real tight, something great (something as great as God himself) begins to rise up in you. At this instant you realize that you were put on the earth for this moment in time - you realize that the impossible is possible! Outside boys! They open the gate. All hell explodes in every direction. Is your God-given dream a blessing or a nightmare? Help God!

Tornado rears up (you need finances for your dream), he goes into a blinding spin (your health and well being are attacked); he sunfishes (people are talking ugly about you for no good reason). He tries to hook you with his horns (your own family comes against you). Your destiny has put you on this impossibility (bull) - no turning back. **Psalm 34**, *"Many are the afflictions (jumps, bucks and spins) of the righteous, but the Lord delivers them out of them all."* When will the whistle blow? You don't think you can last any longer.

Hang on cowboy - *"Greater is He that is in you than he that is in the world."* *"If God be for us, who (or what) can be against us?'* *"I can do all things through Christ who strengthens me!"* The whistle blows - you did it! God did it in and through you. Now, you know Him and love Him like never before. Goliath's head is in your hand! God made you to win.

Freckles on Tornado

The Impossi-bull is possible!

Mark 9:23: *Gods word translation*

...*"everything is possible to him who believes.*

Champions Stay Focused

⚬⚬⚬

If you've ever visited the Cowboy Hall of Fame in Oklahoma City, you've seen the giant bronze statue of Bill Linderman standing with his bronc saddle. Here's a great Bill story.

My dad was rodeoing hard in the fifties, and much of the time he flew to rodeos. One year, dad, his pilot Paul Templeton and Bill Linderman were going hard, working several rodeos at the same time of New York's Madison Square Garden. Working multiple rodeos usually has a common denominator – you're running late! It's going to take a miracle to get there in time.

On this particular day, they were major late flying Paul's small plane into New York's La Guardia Airport. To complicate matters, their radio went out in the transmitting mode. They could hear the air trafficker asking them to identify themselves, but Paul could not respond with his microphone. Remember, they're late, and Bill is up in the bareback riding, which is the first event. So what does Paul do? He gets in the traffic landing pattern with the big jets! "Houston, no, New York, we have a problem."

Meanwhile, Bill has taken out his bareback riggin' and goes through the slow process of taping his riggin' handhold and getting his glove set in place (old time riggin'). Thankfully, the air traffickers decided not to have them shot out of the sky, but make no mistake, they were hot! Really hot! When the cowboys landed, the airport police descended on them like bees on a hive!

Paul, Dad, and Bill got out of the little plane, and Bill had his hand in his glove, which is inside the taped bareback riggin'. Just as the police ran up to them and are about to speak, Bill blurted out, "I ain't got time for this B.S., boys – I'm up in the bareback riding at the Garden!" Guess What? Instead of hauling them off to jail, the police jump all three in the car and hot foot it to Madison Square Garden just in time for Bill to get on his horse! Amazing!

For me, personally, this story speaks several things. Probably the biggest one is that these men were on a mission. They were going to get where they were going one way or another. . and they were willing to do whatever it took to get the job done.

What about your life? Are you on a mission? If you're a Christian, your mission should be to glorify God and fulfill what He has for you to do, and to overcome any obstacle that stands in your way.

Now, I'm not suggesting that we do anything as crazy as the La Guardia episode. However, I've read scripture after scripture where God tells us to live fearless. When we know that God is for us and that He's with us, then we know that He's there to help us in every situation!

I love the story of Nehemiah. It's incredible! God put it in Nehemiah's heart to rebuild Jerusalem. The walls and gates of Jerusalem had been burned and demolished by her enemies. Enter Nehemiah with the help of King Artaxerxes. However, here comes opposition (on steroids) in the form of Tobiah, Sanballat and Geshem. These men used the threats of fear, dread and torment in an effort to stop the mission that Nehemiah was on! Satan is persistent. He brings the same old garbage bag of negative things to try and stop us. Here's a tip. The next time he tells you what you can't do, or that you're going to fail for sure - just tell him, in Jesus' name, "I haven't got time for you!"

"I'M ON A MISSION!"

GO FOR IT!

The Hand Shake

————∞∞∞————

*J*can remember being in Nampa, Idaho at the Snake River Stampede with my dad. He was entered in the bronc riding. I was 13 or 14 years old and had a dream in my heart to be a champion calf roper. However, I had major doubts that I would be big enough.

At that time they roped big calves and almost all the top ropers were big guys: Dean Oliver, Sonny Davis, Mark Shricker, Warren Wuthier. All of them were 6'2" or over, and weighed over 200 lbs.

Before the rodeo one night my dad introduced me to one of my big-time heroes. His name was Jim Bob Altizer - a world champion calf roper from Del Rio, Texas. As I reached out to shake his hand our eyes were level. He's around 5'9" I was his height exactly. The inside of me exploded. "I can do it, I can do it. Jim Bob did - so can I!" It truly ignited my faith to go for my dream. One encounter - do you see it? My life changed in one hand shake! What happened that day? I believe I saw into an unseen realm. The realm where all things are possible!

When you have a dream you have to see past the limitations and impossibilities of this world. When everything cries out that you're crazy to be dreaming so big - you must have your hopes "in the possibility." Jesus said in **Mark 9:23**, *"If you can believe, all things are possible to him that believes."* Getting into that realm may be as simple as a handshake. Whatever it takes; once your faith is activated, you're dream train is going forward on the dream track. Choo choo! I can do it; I can do it, choo, choo. God is with me. God is with me - choo, choo! I can see it! I can see it! Choo Choo Champion!

Years later I was having some major doubts and questions concerning my roping dream. I began to seek God seriously for an answer. I started to fast and pray for a season. You know, sometimes you have to do what it takes to hear from heaven. A few weeks later I was sleeping in my gooseneck trailer at a rodeo in Kalispell, Montana. At 1:00 in the morning the Holy

Spirit woke me as He spoke in my heart, "You keep waiting to see something before you believe it - it doesn't work that way. You have to see it as already done in advance - through the "eyes of faith." The dreams and promises that God gives His people have to be received, appropriated and brought into this earthly realm by faith.

When you can't see a possibility in this world, your faith goes after it in the unseen world and brings it here. When you believe against all odds and continue to believe in the midst of all kinds of adversity, the fulfillment of your dream is in progress. "When I shook hands with Jim Bob that day, I could see my dream through the eyes of faith."

What is your dream champion? Is there something that is causing you to doubt if it can ever happen? I pray that God is going to bring just the right person or thing to you that will activate and ignite your faith. If you agree with that -

"Let's shake on it"

Hebrews 11:1 *(new living), "Faith is the confidence that what we hope for will actually happen; it gives us assurance about things we cannot see."*

II Corinthians 4:18 *(Berean Study Bible), "So we fix our eyes not on what is seen but on what is unseen. For what is seen is temporary, but what is unseen is eternal."*

"Forever Young"
David and Pat Young

John S.O.G.

────── ⚬⚬⚬⚬ ──────

*I*t was the early eighties and Sherry and I were making the long haul from Texas to Alberta, Canada. It was raining in the month of May, and it felt like we were in Alaska in January. As we were driving north of Calgary, the wind was all but blowing over a one-legged hitchhiker on a crutch.

We didn't pick up many hitchhikers but this was an exception. We got him inside our motor home and realized he was big time cold and wet. We talked for a little while and then we asked him what his name was. He said "John Sonofagun." He wasn't smiling so we didn't question the validity of his name. Pretty soon John started speaking some things about our daughter Shandy. She was just a baby then. He began to tell us how God was going to use Shandy in her lifetime. His words were like words of scripture framed in a normal conversation. We had never heard anything quite like it. It was awesome!

As we were going down the road Sherry and I were putting a love basket together for John. Dry clothes, shirt, jacket, cap, some groceries, money and anything else we could think of to send with him. We were coming up on the Olds, Alberta exit where there was a truck stop on the corner. John insisted we let him out on the North bound side of the freeway. This meant he would need to walk across both the north and south-bound lanes to get to the truck stop. Well, we prayed with him and asked the Lord to protect him, and with tears in our eyes away we all went.

We had only gone about 200 feet when we looked back to see John, but he was gone. I mean gone! There were no trees or shrubs to block our view of him. He had simply disappeared. Who was John Sonofagun?

I believe with all my heart that John was an angel. The things he spoke to us and the manner in which he spoke them were like nothing we've ever experienced. Perhaps you have entertained angels and didn't know it. God is visiting us and speaking to us much more than we can comprehend.

Be on the lookout!

Hebrews 13:2 *amp, "Do not forget to extend hospitality to strangers – being friendly, cordial and gracious, sharing the comforts of your home and doing your part generously – for through it some have entertained angels without knowing it."*

Deb Copenhaver

Meeteetsee

*I*t was the mid 1980s, and it was Cowboy Christmas. What is Cowboy Christmas? For pro rodeo cowboys and cowgirls it's the 4th of July, and you may go to 10 rodeos or more in a week's time. Everyone is pumped! If you get "really hot" you could cinch a National Finals Rodeo berth. Sherry and I had just left the Greeley, Colorado rodeo and were on our way to Cody, Wyoming.

It was early morning before daybreak, and the unimaginable happens! Our vehicle quits running. We are broke down somewhere near Meeteetsee, Wyoming. We are on the side of the road with my calf roping horse - wondering what in the world we're going to do now. Almost nothing is as humbling or discouraging as breaking down in the middle of nowhere, let alone at a time like this. What do we do? Did I mention we are close to Meeteetsee? What's a Meeteetsee?

Guess what? We prayed! **Jeremiah 33:3** says, *"Call upon me and I will answer you, and show you great and mighty things which you know not."* What I'm about to tell you is so crazy that I barely believe it - but it's true. Not long after

we prayed, this old semi- truck with a big flat bed trailer pulls up. We tell the driver our predicament and he comes up with an idea that was definitely beyond what our tiny intellects could have dreamed of. He said, "do you want me to load your truck and trailer and horse up on my flat-bed? I have a winch to pull it on with." We said "sure" and then we were slightly stunned as he slowly winched the entire outfit up on to his trailer. Next he chained everything down. There were no side rails! Wow! It looked pretty scary!

Sherry and I got in the cab with the driver and were on our way to Cody, Wyoming. Glory to God! Rock-N-Rodeo! We probably made a mistake when we told the driver that we were in a big hurry because of the time we had lost. Off we go! He cranks this old truck up to almost 80 miles an hour. For whatever reason, he had no mufflers; it roared like a freight train.

Here's the hilarious part. Our driver passes a rodeo rig and Leo Camarillo (World Champion team roper) is sound asleep in the back seat of his truck. With our truck roaring, we honk our horn and wave to Leo, who wakes up in the backseat just as Sherry and I are waving at him. He looks at us, then back at our truck and trailer and from the look on his face, he must have thought he was hallucinating! It was crazy! We make it on to Cody, get a new alternator and then drive to rodeos at Red Lodge and Livingston, Montana. Sherry and I thanked God for being so real and awesome to answer our prayers in such a miraculous way!

What's your predicament? Does your situation seem so impossible and bizarre that you feel there's no point in even praying? You feel stranded in the middle of nowhere without any thread of hope. Jesus loves you and He's waiting for you to ask Him and believe Him to intervene on your behalf! My favorite scripture is **Isaiah 41:10**, *"Fear not for I am with you; do not look around you in terror for I am your God. I will help you."* God promises He will help you in any and every life situation.

Luke 18:1 says, *"Man should always pray and not to faint."* A friend of mine said he spent a good portion of his life trying to overcome a *"spirit of self pity."* When we run into challenging situations we can either "pray and cowboy up (be overcomers) or we can feel sorry for ourselves, becoming angry, bitter and defeated. Winners look to the answer, the way out, the victory instead of focusing on the problem.

NOTHING IS IMPOSSIBLE WITH GOD
GO FOR IT!

Hebrews 4:16 *(amp), "Let us fearlessly and confidently and boldly draw near to the throne of grace (the throne of God's un-merited favor to us sinners), that we may receive mercy (for our failures) and find grace to help in good time for every need (ap-propriate help and well-timed help, coming just when we need it).*

First Nations Rising

*I*t was October 1984 and I was in Gallup, New Mexico teaching a calf roping school. The rodeo complex was called Cowboy World and it was full of Native American Cowboys. For the last three years, I had been conducting clinics at reservations all over North America. As I worked with these young men, I was truly amazed at their athletic abilities and their natural gifting to ride a horse. My encouragement for them was to put the Lord first in their lives, dream big and then work hard to develop the God- given talents they'd been blessed with.

Well, at the end of the school, a 15-year old roper wanted to match me in a 6-head competition. I was 35 at the time and pretty much in my prime but you've got to realize this "young gun" was 15 going on 25. He was fast, consistent, and confident! P.S. Nothing could please this young guy more than beating the "instructor". Well, without going into detail, I can tell you that I had a tiger by the tail. On 6 calves, I won the match by less than 2 seconds. I had to rope my tail off to barely beat this teenage champion! Wow! I was so impressed by him. The next night I roped at the pro rodeo in Oklahoma City. As I rode into the box to compete all I could think of was "Thank God, I'm not roping against that kid tonight! Today the greatness that I saw in that young cowboy is exploding in rodeo. The time is now for "First Nations" people and it's exciting to watch!

Billy Graham spoke at the Chief conference in Albuquerque, New Mexico in 1975. He said, "You as Native Americans are a sleeping giant. The original Americans, you are now awakening! Just around the corner you may become a spiritual superpower in this country that could change not only America, but the world!"

First Nations cowboy
Ted Nuce "1985 world
champion bull rider"

Ted Nuce says, "It's always very exciting to me to see guys that find their passion in life and really raise the bar. I am very proud of Derek Begay, Dustin Bird, Aaron Tsinigine, Erich Rogers, Ryan Dirteater, and so many others. Every champion knows exactly how important it is to overcome all the negative things along the journey. When you learn to overcome is when you become a champion!" The Bible says in Phillipians 4:13 "I can do all things through Christ who gives me strength."

Can you see it?! First Nations people rising like a giant eagle becoming the champions God created them to be and then declaring the glory of His only begotten son!

Toots Boots

⸎

One of the great champions in rodeo was Toots Mansfield. He was a 7 time world champion calf roper. As a boy, I can remember the calf roping book that Toots wrote. It was great! Toots was not only a great roper, but he was also hard to beat in a foot race. For several years at Denver all the Texas cowboys would bring extra cash to bet on "the race." The Northern cowboys would bring the fastest guy they could find every year. However, no one could ever come close to beating him.

Watching Toots trounce them every year and take their money evidently got a little monotonous - let alone costly. So they came up with a plan. They found a sprinter from the University of Colorado who could "fly"!. Hold it! This race was supposed to be between the cowboys. Right? Toots didn't say anything. The runners were to start from the back of the roping and bull-dogging boxes. The Colorado sprinter wore sprint clothes with track shoes. Toots just had his cowboy clothes, jeans and boots. However, just before they got ready to run, Toots did something he had never done through the years. He took his boots off! Evidently, the competition he was facing was forcing him to extreme measures! Socks only. Off they go like rockets! A cowboy and a track star. How about this? Toots beat him by one yard. He must have been like lightning! I'm not sure about this but I'm guessing that probably ended the annual foot race.

I was speaking at a church recently and was telling this story. Then I took my boots off and started running as fast as I could go. I said, "It's time, believers, that we pick up the pace. We need to do what God has called us to do with all the gusto we can."

Before Jesus left the earth He gave all believers a mandate. Go (run) into all the world and share the good news to everyone. Question: who or what does your world consist of? Are you praying for your family, fellow workers, and friends? Are you consciously reaching out to people with the love of Jesus?

God truly wants you to win! Kick your boots off and go a little faster!

GO (run) FOR IT!

Hebrews 12:1, *(msg)*, *"Do you see what this means - all these pioneers who blazed the way, all these veterans cheering us on? It means we'd better get on with it. Strip down, start running - and never quit! No extra spiritual fat, no parasitic sins, Keep your eyes on Jesus, who both began and finished the race we're in."*

Prov. 11:30 *(amp)*,*" The fruit of the [uncompromisingly] righteous is a tree of life, And he who is wise captures and wins souls [for God—he gathers them for eternity]."*

The Herd

∞

Having a calf roper tell you about the special horses he's owned would be like asking NASCAR racer Jeff Gordon about his progression of racing machines. Basically every horse I owned took me a little higher up the ladder.

Buddy was 12 years old and so was I. My Dad bought him in Texas from Buddy Groff (a runner-up world champion calf roper). He was a pretty sorrel and was truly my Buddy. Then came Brownie - a dark brown with a black mane and tail. He was a little bit hyper, but I thought it was great! Then came Sam. He was reddish brown and he was faster than the first two. Next on the horse list was Powder, who was the epitome of his name - pure white like baby powder. He could stop like a car hitting a brick wall at 40 mph. My next horse was Paint, and he was pro material, the real thing. He had a big white spot on his left rib that technically made him paint. I bought J.L. from my friend and great cowboy Buzz Peth. He was a yellow sorrel and I went to my first National Finals Rodeo on him. My life long dream of being a World Champion came true riding Streak; a beautiful copper-penny, red sorrel. I bought him from my friend Terry Reiter, who trained him. (Terry was recently inducted into the Idaho Cowboy Hall of Fame) Little kids would run up to me and say, "Boy! That's a pretty horse mister!" The cover picture shows me riding Sugar. He might have been my favorite horse when he was working good. One of my last horses was Glory! He got killed on a freeway by Abilene, Texas. My wife Sherry prayed and cried over Glory. He was jet black! He could fly. Someday, we'll get to see him again in heaven.

All these horses were different . . . different colors, confirmations, dispositions and abilities. Did I love all of them? You bet! Let me ask you this? Horses are God's creations, right? What about us? . . . the human race - white, black, brown, yellow and all shades in between. What a diversity of different people living in different places with different life styles, customs, giftings and talents. Yet, just like the diversity of horses that complimented each other and led to an ultimate end, such is the case with all races of people.

Scripture tells us that all of God's creation is perfectly and wonderfully made. (**Psalm 139:14**); and that mankind is made in God's very image. (**Genesis 1:26**) With this in mind how can we question the value or beauty of another human being? How could I say Brownie was no good because of his color? Was Powder too white? Was Streak's shiny penny too copper? Was Glory too black? Do paints have too many colors? God forbid! Actually, He does forbid- He says, "Judge not lest you be judged." (**Matthew 7:1**)

Has someone in your past (family or friends) sown the seed of prejudice in your life? If so, you need first of all to forgive them; then ask the Lord to forgive you for picking up that awful spirit of racial hatred. Tell the Lord, "Jesus, I refuse to allow this to live in my life." God has a large diversified family and He loves all of His creation.

I loved all my horses and they helped me become a champion. Let's love all of our brothers and sisters and help one another become His champions.

GO FOR IT!

John 13:35 *(amp), "By this shall all (men) know that you are My disciples, if you love one another (if you keep on showing love among yourselves)."*

Romans 2:11 *(amp) "For God shows no partiality [no arbitrary favoritism; with Him one person is not more important than another]."*

Jeff on Brownie

Champions Expect the Best

———— ⌘ ————

few years ago I was roping some practice calves here at my arena in Granbury, Texas. I had been tying several calves in the 9-second range. As I rode back to the roping chute, the Holy Spirit spoke in my heart, "You're not putting your heart into it." I realized as soon as He said it that I had quit expecting the best I could do. I backed into the box and roped my next calf in 8.0 seconds. What was the difference between the 9-second runs and the 8-second run? On the latter run, I threw myself into it because I expected the best.

Hebrews 11:1, *"Now faith is the substance of things we hope for. (or expect)"* If we don't have great expectations then we have nothing to apply our faith to. Everyone has the choice of living by faith, or living in doubt and unbelief - afraid to launch out into what seems totally impossible.

Did you see the movie Hoosiers - a classic true story of a high school basketball team in Indiana? They made it to the state championship game against a much, much bigger school. With just a few seconds left in the game the Cinderella team had the ball with a chance to win. The coach called a play in the huddle with the ball going to one of the players who wasn't the star. The players just stood there not saying anything. The coach said, "What's the matter with you guys?" Finally, very humble yet confident their star player said, "I'll make it." The coach changed the play and their star player got the ball and scored. He had expectations that he was ready to put action (faith) to.

Are you suffering from sickness or disease of some kind? Expect to be healed, and then turn a real living active faith loose to see it come to pass. Don't just say, "I hope God will heal me." If you expect it, then let your faith pull on God till you see the manifestation in your body. **Isaiah 53:5** and **I Peter 2:24** read, *"by His stripes you are healed."* The lady with the deadly blood disease in the bible said, *"If I can just grab the hem of His garment. . ."* Her faith grabbed God and pulled on Him, and she received her healing. But first, she had to expect it.

Are you expecting a better income? Well, if you really are, then pull on God for His creativity and direction for your life. Maybe you need to quit your (good) job and start the business that's been in your heart for a long time. Expect it to succeed. Don't let doubt and fear cheat you out of it.

Not long ago I was playing a pretty bad round of golf. On a par three hole, my ball was about 20 feet off the green and 50 feet from the hole. In my spirit the Lord spoke to me, "Shoot to make it, not to just get close." With that, I approached the shot with much more focus, concentration and confidence. I hit the shot, it jumped on the green and as it got closer to the hole I could see it was going to be close. Well, down it went! All right! See, God doesn't just want you to get close; He wants you to win!

Expect the blessing of God in your life. Faith in God can make the impossible possible; but first you've got to expect it. What you expect controls your attitude, your perspective, and your corresponding faith action. God wants you to experience His very best.

Champions Expect the Best!

Go for It!

From the movie, *"Hoosiers"*

White Horse, White Calf

ere's another 1975 travel story that I prob ably wouldn't even believe myself, if it weren't true. It was October, and the championship race was really close. I flew from California to Tulsa and from Tulsa to Atlanta. I was trying to get to the rodeo in Bonifay, Florida by 8:00 PM that night. Well, I found out my commercial flight was cancelled from Atlanta to somewhere in Florida. So I had to charter a private plane.

As we were flying across Florida we found out that most of the airport landing lights were destroyed by a hurricane that had hit Northern Florida. Since we couldn't land in Bonifay, things got complicated. We continued to fly and look for an airport with lights. Finally we headed for Marianna, Florida. By now we are almost out of gas and its dark - not a good combination. By the time we landed at Marianna our gas gauge was pegged out. Thank God; we're on land.

I called a taxi and away we went. I think it was around 45 minutes to Bonifay. I told the cab driver my whole rodeo story in an effort to get him to drive fast. The problem was his wife was with him; and about the time we'd start going faster, she would loudly remind him that he just got another ticket and if he got any more he would lose his license. I couldn't believe it . . I'd get him going faster, and she'd slow him down. This went on for almost an hour till we got there. On arriving in Bonifay, I jumped out of the cab and started running toward the lights of the rodeo arena. They were roping calves already, and I didn't have a clue what horse I was going to ride. I was thankful that I wasn't one of the first four ropers, or I would have been too late.

I got my rope and string out of my rope can as I asked a roper with a nice looking white horse if I could get a ride. He said yes and I jumped on. I had no idea what kind of calf I had drawn, but as I rode into the box I saw a bright white brahma calf with about a four-inch hump on his back. He looked like a junior PBR wanna be. It was not at all what I was hoping to see - but, here we go - white horse, white calf. I roped him fairly quick and flanked him quick enough to win something. That's where it ended- he kicked and kicked and kicked - I think he's still kicking! I got the whistle. No time. Game over.

Now I'm looking for my cab driver and his wife. They're gone. I'm sure the wife was tired of me; we had that in common. So, now I've got to find a ride back to Marianna. It was the middle of the night when I finally got back to the plane. My pilot had slept in the plane while I was gone; and about two in the morning we arrived back in Atlanta five minutes too late to catch my flight to California. This was the last flight out to allow me to compete at rodeos in Stockton, Visalia and Costa Mesa. Was this devastating? Almost! WOW! Did things turn out the way I'd hoped? No! Did I give it my best? Yes!

Isn't it amazing what happens (good and bad) when you launch out on a faith adventure? As long as you play it safe (not pursuing your dream) there will be minimal challenges. It's like comparing a life in the wading pool as opposed to launching down faith's river rapids. The joy and excitement in the river is the discovery that God is awesome and mighty to back you up, go before you, and be with you in every situation. Hurricanes, landing lights, taxi drivers, their wives, white calves, and departing airplanes – so what! Keep your head up – God wants you to win!

GO FOR IT!

Heb 10:36 *(amp), "Do not, therefore, fling away your fearless confidence, for it carries a great and glorious compensation of reward."*

Hayley Danley
"When you're not winning, pass the test by taking It gracefully."
Favorite scripture II Chronicles 15:7

Getting Your Fight Back

───❊❊❊───

t was 1974 and I was in the middle of pursuing my life-long dream of being a world champion calf roper. I was riding into the roping box at an indoor arena in Seaside, Oregon and I was breathing hard from the runs I had just made. Rope burns, calf manure and arena dirt decorated my body. For over three months I had roped over 100 calves a day going at every run as hard as I could go. I roped somewhere in the range of 10,000 calves I was exhausted, but I loved every minute of it; however, make no mistake, it was a fight.

After about three or four thousand calves into this rope-a-thon, I went to the pro rodeo at Puyallup, Washington. It was a long rodeo and we competed on seven calves. I won 6 of those go-rounds and the average. I was pumped!

As you pursue your dreams and experience the great life that God has for you; you will run into challenges and difficulties that will try to stop you and tempt you to quit. You'll have to rise up and fight! Jesus said, "In this world you will have tribulation; but be of good cheer for I have overcome them." As born again believers, we overcome by walking in the victory that Jesus gained for us. He defeated death, hell, and the grave. Now we overcome by rising up in our spirit-man and fighting the good fight. (Standing on God's promises.) We walk by faith and not by what we see; and we learn to follow the leading of the Holy Spirit!

I was roping at my friend's house not long after I had double hip replacement. My hips were fine but I realized that the rotator cuff in my right shoulder was almost non-existent. I tried to rope a couple of calves with no success. Two misses. As I was riding to the other end of the arena to bring the calves back, I told my friend, "You know, sometimes we just need to get mad!" I ran my next two calves and roped each of them in two swings {Even though my arm was barely able to throw a rope.} A holy anger, a fighting spirit helped me accomplish what I was trying to do.

Have life's circumstances blind-sided you and caused you to lie down; hunkered up in a ball? You're tired physically, mentally, emotionally and spiritually. Have you quit pursing your dream? Are you in prison and given up on life? Paul wrote two thirds of the new testament while he was in jail. Is your marriage fading? Are you getting fat and growing old prematurely? Are things tough financially and you're tired of fighting it? I have a word for you from heaven! Straight from your heavenly Fathers heart! GET YOUR FIGHT BACK! Rise up and use the name that is above every name; the powerful wonderful name of Jesus. Then begin to take positive steps of faith in a winning direction. You may not see it now in your natural circumstances; but victory is on the horizon! Are you like the mouse caught in the trap? You don't want the cheese anymore; you just want out of the trap. You've lost your fight - that inner desire to resist, overcome hardships, and stand up for what you believe.

If you had your fight back you would put one foot in front of the other and keep on keeping on. Exodus 15:3 says: God is a man of war. Well, if He lives in you -what does that make you? You are a man of war or a woman of war! - A soldier in the Kings army. What do soldiers do? They fight! Call on the name of Jesus. He will resurrect you! He will give you your hope back, your strength back, your joy back; YOUR FIGHT BACK!

Olympic gold medal runner Wilma Rudolph said, "If you can pick up after a crushing defeat and go on to win again, you are going to be a champion someday." What do you do after a crushing defeat?

They asked William Wallace in Brave heart: "where are you going?" As he was riding into the battle, he said, " I'm going to pick a fight." There's something regal about getting your fight back. What does "fight" mean? It means to oppose evil - it means resisting the very thing that was meant to destroy you. It means facing the giant that would keep you from accomplishing God's will for your life, and entering into your Promised Land! Isn't it time to blow the dust off your God-driven dream and get your fight back?!

GO FOR IT!

I Tim. 6:12 (amp) -" Fight the good fight of faith; take hold of the eternal life to which you were called.

Matt 11:12 (ASV), "And from the days of John the Baptist until the present time, the kingdom of heaven has endured violent assault, and violent men seize it by force.

Jeff on
bucking colt
age 10

Grizzly For God

———— ∞∞∞ ————

Did you ever get around a campfire as a kid at church camp or on a weekend campout? Before the fire went out someone started telling bear stories. We're not talking about the 3 bears here, folks,; these were bear (eating-people) stories. By the time the fire went out the little kids were usually shaking in their boots.

Our special friends the Eversons lived in Alaska for several years. Recently, Carl gave me a book called "Alaska Bear Tales." Wow, you should hear some of the wild stories about the Alaskan Kodiak brown bear, which is the largest species of the grizzly bear. These bears are literally monstrous in size, strength and ferocity. For three days in a row, I would read stories to Sherry and Shandy (my wife and daughter) about these bears mauling people, moose and other animals. Finally, Shandy said, "enough already, it's too gory!" Well, I admit it was pretty gory! I guess what fascinated me, though, was the incredible power that these animals have. It makes me think of the unlimited power of God.

Men, did you know according to **Eph. 5:22**, God puts the husband in the position of Christ (God) in the marriage? Husbands love your wives like Christ loved the church. All the power of the universe now resides in you. Not only that, but when you receive Jesus as your Lord and Savior you received God Himself into your life. Also, when the power of the Holy Spirit comes in your life according to **Acts 1:8**, God's very own anointing and ability are yours. However, with this power and authority comes tremendous responsibility. With this in mind, men, take a journey with me. I want you to look at yourself as a giant Kodiak "grizzly" bear.

Did you know some bears are almost 13' tall? God wants the people in your life to be able to look up to you for wisdom, courage, strength and stability just like the Kodiak bear. Have you ever read about David's soldiers called the "mighty men of valor" in **I Chronicles 11:10-47**? These men were truly "Kodiaks for God." One man killed 800 men in battle single-handedly. God wants you to stand tall and become the man that He created you to be. As you come to know the God who lives in you, He wants you to be victorious against all kinds of sin - pornography, lust, greed, selfishness, laziness, pride, arrogance, compromise, and every sort of disobedience to God.

Ah, but there are two sides to every coin. No one would want to live with a ferocious grizzly every day. Just as the Bible says, "God is a man of war, (**Ex 15:13**) - He is also love". (I John 4:8), If you want to know about love you have to meet God Himself. WOW! You mean the grizzly has a tender, sensitive, loving, compassionate, merciful side? Exactly! You've got it!

Men, are you fighting and being ferocious with those you love - your wife, children, family and friends? Jesus could have hated the world for crucifying Him, but instead He loved them! He said as He died, "Father, forgive them for they know not what they do." Are you forgiving, soft spoken and kind on a consistent basis? If you aren't, God help the household, the "grizzly is on the rampage"! He's tearing up the house. "Grizzlies, ah, I mean men," it's so inappropriate for you to vent your anger and frustrations toward your family. You're supposed to be the strength, the foundation, and the encouragement in your household - not the destruction!

Now, here is what the Holy Spirit showed me. Picture this - a huge killing-machine weighing 1500 lbs. with 6 inch long claws, gently stroking the wings of a butterfly. That's you men! Are you getting the vision yet? Tough, in a good God way. A man that hates compromise and unholiness. A man that lives ferocious with a cause for God and yet to know him is to know a "big mush" in the heart. A man that wants to comfort, encourage, befriend and heal those around him. Do you see it? If you do, you can become that "grizzly for God" - the tough and tender giant. Read God's Word and then do it. You will begin to see these "grizzly" qualities develop in you.

"Grrr FOR IT!"

Here Comes Bill

A friend of mine that plays real good golf says this about my game. "You've got great potential; you just need to draw it out." I've never really known how to take that comment; as a compliment or a slam. I always end up choosing to take it as a challenge to do my best. Either way the statement is true. We all have gifts and talents that give us great potential. The question is, "can we draw them out"– especially when we run into big obstacles?

I love this story. My dad and Bill Linderman were rodeoing at Chicago in the fifties. There were three go-rounds in the saddle bronc riding and Dad had ridden two of his horses; he was sitting real good in the average. In the meantime, it was several days before he would compete again, and he got the flu. There was a strain of flu going around called the Asian flu. Some people were dying from it. Dad said he never left the motel room and continued to get sicker and sicker. Well, the big night came, and he had drawn a horse named Fashion Plate that was about as good as horses get. Bill was staying with Dad who was lying in bed considering dying as a comforting option. Bill said to him, "get up, it's time to go to the rodeo." Dad said something like "I just can't do it. I'm too sick, it's not going to happen!" Bill must have known this was going to take drastic measures. Dad said Bill back handed him across the jaw so hard that it almost knocked him out. Now, Dad had to decide if he was going to face the flu and go to the rodeo, or face Bill. Dad chose the former!

He said getting out of bed and putting his clothes on felt like climbing Mt. Everest. Imagine being that sick and then getting on a rank bucking horse. Well, the "Paul Harvey" (the rest of the story) is that he rode Fashion Plate that night and scored a

196 under the old 200-point marking system and won Chicago.

One of my all time favorite scriptures is Proverbs 23:17 which says, "As iron sharpens iron, so a man sharpens the countenance of his friend." We all have great potential, but we need a friend like Bill to draw it out. Sometimes we need someone to sympathize with us in our misery, but we also need friends like Bill that challenge us and wake us up to the moment. Bill knew that Dad was capable of a great ride.

Guess what? So are you! You have the potential to be a champion in your world with your God-given abilities. Are you lying in a prison bed thinking your mistakes have disqualified you from life's game – sinking into a pool of self pity? Maybe you are going through physical pain and sickness like dad, and you just can't see yourself coming out on the other side. Are you down and out financially and almost too tired to fight it anymore? Well, get ready! Here comes Bill. He's walking up to your bed of affliction – whack! He backhands you. Wow, that was hard! Now it's time to get up and put your pants on; you are His champion, the best God's got.

Bill Linderman
Cowboy
Hall of Fame

HAVE A GREAT RIDE!

Ship Shape

⊷⊶⊷

When No One is Watching

My special friend Leon Clift at one time was the bass player for Roger Miller, and the opening act for Diana Ross and the Supremes, and also for the doors. He is truly a champion in the music world; but what I appreciate most about Leon is his friendship and character. He has worked with our ministry for several years now and has truly been a blessing. He is a man of integrity. I love this story in Leon's own words:

I was 18 years old, right out of Navy Boot Camp and just stationed in the Navy at the Pearl Harbor military station in Hawaii. I had dreams of great things to come. I was immediately placed on K P Duty (washing dishes etc. for the station). It was a small area, with room to hold all the dirty dishes and pans. (not what I had dreamed of). What a letdown! Joining the Navy to see the world and seeing instead a world of dirty dishes. I guessed my dream had been detoured somehow; so, I decided to do my best where I was.

I began to clean up the whole area in which I had been placed - to do my best in a bad situation. I swept and mopped the floor and polished all the old brass fixtures and cleaned the windows. I know I was put there to wash dirty dishes but; I decided to go the extra mile. This went on for a couple of months till one day it was inspection time from the company commander.

Nervously, I stood by at attention as he walked into "my area" of responsibility. He looked around, placing his white gloved hands over different things and then looked at his hands. Then my heart sank as he exclaimed, "who is in charge of this place?!" The eyes of the other officers behind him got big and looked at me. Not knowing what to expect, I said, "I am sir!" He looked at me very sternly and said something no one expected

- "get this sailor out of here, and promote him to assistant chief master at arms! I'm looking for men like this who do their best when no one is watching!" WOW! My situation had changed for the better! Because I had chosen to be honorable and make the best out of a bad situation, God had chosen to bless me.

My friends, God is with you all the time; and He is watching how you deal with hard times. Can you maintain a good attitude during difficult circumstances? Things not going well for you? Your attitude will determine your altitude! Someone has said, "Dance like no one is watching, sing like no one is listening. "

Anchors A Weigh Champion!

Personal story by Leon Clift

Daniel 6:3 *(ASV)," Then this Daniel was distinguished above the presidents and the satraps, because an excellent spirit was in him, and the king thought to set him over the whole realm."*

From Sailor...
...to Singer.

Sierra!

―――∞∞∞―――

"Time to go girl!"

by Sherry Copenhaver

Years ago Jeff's dad gave our daughter, Shandy, a beautiful black mare named Sierra. She is a part of our family. She has raised us some awesome colts and in the truest sense of the word; she is priceless. It was going to be another typical hot summer day in August and Jeff had gone down the road to feed grain to our horses that were turned out on summer pasture. Now, these guys know their routine; and when you get there at 7:30 AM they are all standing at their buckets anticipating their grain. Except that morning - my old buckskin and an older pony were there, but not our really nice black mare (and they are always together). So out in the pasture Jeff went calling Sierra. Finally about 200 feet away there she stood - frozen - not moving a lick. Jeff kept calling her and upon walking up to her, he saw why she wasn't moving. As you can see in the picture she had all the flesh from the top front part of her right leg stripped down and was laying open with the huge muscle that causes her to move forward - hanging down. Why she had not bled to death was a miracle.

I'm at home when Jeff calls me and said, "Sherry, it's awful. You better call the vet and come down now." Almost immediately the Holy Spirit spoke to him and said - NO - don't say that; it's not awful - speak (say) that it's "do-able." Wow! Talk about the instantaneous power of "life and death in the tongue." **Prov.18:21**, amp *"Death and life are in the power of the tongue, and they who indulge in it shall eat the fruit of it."* We can either agree with the circumstances as they are, etc. or we can choose to agree with God.

I immediately called our good friend, Dr. Wayne Howell -

the best vet on the planet (in my opinion) who said he would be there within the hour. Well at that point, it seemed like an eternity. When I got down the road to the horses, Jeff had managed to coax Sierra closer to the other horses out in the open. I took one look at her and a thousand thoughts hit my mind: this is too bad to fix; she'll never walk again; even if she does she'll be a cripple; and this is it, you'll have to put her down! But I knew not to speak it - only believe, only believe and you will see the glory of God. When Doc arrived he knew we would have to work on her in the pasture. When he got to her; he did not say a word either - he just looked at me and said "you'll need a miracle." Jeff and I knew who was in the miracle working business. We all joined hands and agreed in prayer for healing and help for Doc as he operated on her. **Matt 18:19** (asv), *"Again I say unto you, that if two of you shall agree on earth as touching anything that they shall ask, it shall be done for them of my Father who is in heaven."* Then Doc went to work.

He had to cut off that whole chunk of muscle and flesh in order to proceed because he said it was useless to her. He began to do all he could in an impossible situation to help save the leg. Two hours later he stepped back and he said, "now Sherry, we need that miracle.! One of 3 things is going to happen. #1 - she is not going to move forward at all; and that will not be good. #2 - She will move forward and swing her leg out because she now has no forward motion muscle (it's laying in the pasture); and #3 - she will just walk off and we will have our miracle." I took her by the halter, gave her a loving pat (she is a doll) and said, "time to go girl." Guess what happened? She just took off following me - walking straight as an arrow, using that leg like nothing had ever happened. We all just lost it!!

As we led her she stepped forward looking completely normal. Dr. Howell bent over like someone belly punched him. It's a miracle! We spent literally months doctoring her daily. Did you know that God loves us and those things that are dear to us? Doc would come out and check her periodically. On one trip he told us: "the mare's ability to move normally is laying out there in the field." He was referring to that large piece of muscle that had been hanging off her leg. In the natural- she just

wasn't supposed to be walking and running normally.

Looking back at this whole story, I see several dynamic principles at work. #1- our immediate response to life situations is crucial. You can speak life or death. Jesus said (in **Mark 11:23**) that we can truly have what we say. **Job 22:28** says, *"You shall also decree a thing, and it shall be established unto you."* #2 prayer works - and the first part of that prayer was answered when a gifted experienced veterinarian showed up on the scene. God uses people to answer many of our prayers. # 3 - God is awesome! **Jeremiah 33:3** says, *"Call unto me and I will answer you and show you great and mighty things which you know not." When man has done all that he can do; it's not over till God does all He can do."* It's called faith!

Are you faced with a life challenge that needs a miracle? Step forward for victory. Speak life - pray - seek His talented people and believe with all your heart!

GO FOR IT!

Malachi 4:2 *(The Message), "The Sun of Righteousness will dawn on those who honor my name, healing radiating from its wings. You will be bursting with energy, like colts frisky and frolicking.*

You Ain't

———⌘———

Rdeo legend Toots Mansfield was truly a champion example to cowboys in his era. He lived at a time when there were not many confessing Christians in rodeo. Today a big percentage of cowboys and cowgirls have a personal relationship with Jesus Christ! I was talking to rodeo great Clifton Smith the other day and he told me this story about Toots.

A fellow competitor and a top roper himself walked up to Toots at a slack competition at about 9 am in the morning. He got right in Toots' face and said, " I've been out partying and carousing most of the night. I've got a hangover and a headache. How in the world am I going to beat you?" Toots was not only a 7-time world champion, but a man of few words. He looked at this guy, hesitated for just a second and said, "You aint." I enjoy his answer for these reasons. (#1) Toots was confident because he worked hard at his trade. (#2) He knew that his lifestyle didn't hinder his ability to compete at the optimum level.

In the 4th chapter of Matthew, Jesus was led by the spirit to be tempted of the devil. He had fasted for 40 days and satan tempted Him to turn stones into bread. Then satan told Him to jump off a cliff. Then he took Jesus to a high place and showed Him all the kingdoms of the world and the glory of them; and offered them to Him. Each time Jesus responded with the Word of God telling satan "it is written." Basically satan was saying to Jesus: when am I going to beat you with my seduction, lies, and temptations? Mind if I give you the "Toots" translation? Jesus said, "satan—you aint."

Just a few months after Sherry and I gave our lives to Jesus, I was excited to tell my dad I was born again. My dad listened to all I had to say and then said, "don't get on your soap box. I'll watch your life for the next year and see what I see." The way he said it made me realize that he would be watching my life carefully. I knew then that my walk with the Lord could be the difference in him coming to the Lord or not. At the same time, I felt satan's presence saying: "Hey Jeff, when am I going to see you not so excited about Jesus? When am I going to see you go back to the life you used to live?" My answer was short and sweet - "You aint!"

How about you believer? Are you ready to battle the enemy with scripture? **1 Peter 5:8** (new living). *"Stay alert! Watch out, for your great enemy, the devil, prowls around like a roaring lion looking for someone to devour."* Now your adversary says, "When am I going to see you go back into the world? (Living a life of partying, drugs and worthless pursuits?)

OK champion, here we go - I see you cock your head, squint your eyes a little (like Toots) look squarely at your adversary and say...YOU AINT!

GO FOR IT!

Eph 4:26-27 *(ASV): "Be angry, and sin not: let not the sun go down upon your wrath; neither give place to the devil."*

Jeff and Deb in the Panhandle of Texas.

God's Financial Plan
for Champions

———∞∞∞———

In December of 1975, I drove out of Oklahoma City as the newly crowned World Champion Calf Roper. I remember it well. It had been a long, hard year, and I was happy to see a life-long ambition fulfilled. However, like Paul Harvey says, "now for the rest of the story." Pulling out of town, I remember it was drizzling almost frozen rain. I was tired, my horse was tired and the truck that I had bought that year was almost worn out. The Winston bonus money I had won only broke me even financially for the year. How about that... the champion only breaks even! I began to look for something more than rodeo for happiness and personal fulfillment.

I rodeoed enough to finish in the top ten in 1976, then I basically quit in 1977. That same year I met Sherry, the special lady that I've been married to for over 30 years. In June 1978, a couple in Ft. Worth, Texas told us about Jesus Christ. We knelt down and gave our lives to Him that night at the foot of our bed. As we began to read God's Word, the Lord changed our lives step by step. In the summer of 1978, I remember reading in the book of Malachi (the last book of the Old Testament) about tithing.

Now, the word tithe means tenth. Tithing means to bring one tenth or ten percent of your income to God. I had heard people talk about tithing before and after I became a Christian. For some reason I thought it was just something that people had come up with to get your money . . . a religious con game of some kind.

Malachi, starting at the third chapter, verses 7 – 12 says, *"Yet from the days of your fathers, you have gone away from My ordinances and have not kept them. Return to Me, and I will return to you, says the Lord of hosts. But you said, 'In what way shall we return?'*

Will a man rob God? Yet you have robbed Me! But you say, 'In what way have we robbed you?' In tithes and offerings. You are cursed with a curse, for you have robbed Me, even this whole nation. Bring all the tithes into the store house, that there may be food in My house, and try Me now in this," says the Lord of hosts, "If I will not open for you the windows of heaven and pour out for you such a blessing that there will not be room enough to receive it. And I will rebuke the devourer for your sakes, and the nations will call you blessed for you will be a delightful land," says the Lord of hosts.

What a great deal!--God's financial plan for the prosperity and blessing of His children. We bring tithes and offerings to the local church and ministries that the Lord uses to grow us spiritually, and then He does all that He says He will do in His Word. Let me explain something here: #1 - God is not in the cursing business. When we don't tithe, we are opening the door to our enemy (satan) #2 - we have removed ourselves from the blessing through disobedience.

In the fall of 1978 I had already qualified for the NFR, but I hadn't won anything for a few rodeos. Then I won the rodeo at Yakima, Washington in October, it paid approximately $800. Sherry and I wanted to obey God's Word. As we began to go down the needs we had and bills that had to be paid, we realized that we didn't have the $80 left to tithe. I remember thinking to God, "I would like to pay the $80, but as You can see, Lord I will have no money left.

I'm standing there looking up to God with my empty pockets pulled out saying "sorry God." Then the Lord showed me a picture of what was happening. As I looked up to Him with empty pockets, He was looking down at me also holding empty pockets saying, "Sorry Jeff." The scripture He gave me besides **Malachi 3:7-12** was **Galatians 6:7**, *"Be not deceived, God is not mocked, whatever a man sows that shall he also reap."*

We wanted God's blessing in our lives. So Sherry and I began to re-do our budget. We gave God the first ten percent then paid our bills, etc. after that. We have been tithing and giving offerings for over 30 years now. The Lord brought us out of much debt, blessed us with a great marriage, a precious daughter, and son-in-law, two awesome granddaughters, a wonderful place to live, and the good health to enjoy it all.

I can tell you first hand I would rather have the blessings that come from obedience to God's Word than the rewards of being the world's champion. God has a great financial plan for you -He wants you to win!

GO FOR IT!

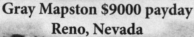
**Gray Mapston $9000 payday
Reno, Nevada**

**Becky Mapston
Mrs. Montana
competing for
Mrs. America
Las Vegas, Nevada**

Camper Crawler

⸿⸿⸿

This true story is so crazy it should have been called "The Three Stooges Go Rodeoing." When my friend Mark Cain told us this story I thought we would injure ourselves; we were laughing so hard. Here we go: Four guys were rodeoing. They were leaving a truck stop, and for some reason, they assumed their fourth friend had gotten in the back of the camper. The truth is, he was walking toward the truck as it began to leave without him. He ran as hard as he could and made it to the back bumper. He was hanging on to the camper door while he was trying to get the driver's attention. No success. Now, the truck began to speed up as they were heading toward the freeway. At this point the fourth cowboy gets an idea! Scary! He decided to crawl onto the top of the camper and crawl over the front to the windshield of the truck. Hold it; you're going to do what? Well, there he goes.

They're going approximately 50 mph and he's crawling forward on the camper. On a danger scale of 1 to 10, this has to be about a 17. So far so good. However, he gets to the front unscathed and then reaches his hand down over the front of the windshield. That'll slow 'em down, right? Now let me interject this, what would you do if you were driving down the road, and a hand appeared in front of you through the windshield? You guessed it! You would slam on the brakes, and so did our driver. Our camper crawler was catapulted forward like a rocket. As the driver is about to get the truck and horse trailer to a complete stop, he was probably thinking he had run over and killed his friend. Guess what! The truck had a deer-guard bumper and our partner got hold of it on his fast-forward slide; his legs were dragging underneath like an "Indiana Jones" scene.

I was lying in bed thinking about this story the other day and started to laugh. Ever so quietly I felt the Holy Spirit speak in my heart, "some choices we make in life are better than others."

That's for sure! Can you believe that he lived through this adventure? It's called the mercy of God. What is mercy? Here's a partial definition, "God protecting and looking out for us when we deserve much worse." When our ignorance or arrogance linked with no good judgment at all could have brought total ruin, the mercy of God is there to make things much better. **Romans 3:23** says we have all sinned and come short of the glory of God. We all do "3 stooges things." They may not be as obvious or as dangerous as the cowboy camper crawler, but we're still guilty.

I believe one of the keys of mercy is "what do you do, when you know His mercy and loving kindness have kept you out of big trouble, big tragedy or big loss?" Do you just go on and pretend you're superman, you're bullet proof, and nothing bad can happen to you? Or do you go to Him in prayer and tell Him, "Thank you Lord for your mercy! Forgive me for doing something so stupid - so void of good judgment. Help me Lord to recognize my need for your protection, wisdom, favor and direction. Thank you Lord for your mercy today in my life!"

GOD WANTS YOU TO WIN!

Ephesians 2:4 *(niv)*, *"But because of his great love for us, God, who is rich in mercy, made us alive with Christ . . . ."*

Training Champions

―∞∞∞―

*I*n September of 2009, an incredible event took place for Sherry and me. Was it a $20 million lottery win; or a Nobel peace prize? No, much, much bigger than that, we became GRAND PARENTS! WOW! Little did we know the awesome joy and fun we were in for; it's hard to even describe it if you've never been there. Our daughter Shandy and her husband, Cody, are really wonderful parents. You can see their love for the Lord poured into their daughters Chloe and Heidi.

Shandy and her girls are not only mom and daughters; they are also best friends. It's amazing how unique the girls are. Chloe loves running, gymnastics and sports. Heidi loves singing, dancing (ballet) and dress up. Both girls have an incredible sense of humor and a zeal for life! The Lord also showed Shandy that this was her ministry - to train their girls to be champions for the Lord.

Probably the most underrated champions in the world are the moms and dads and grandpas and grandmas that give themselves unselfishly to their children. They help them become all that God has for them to be. They are constantly sowing seeds of love into the ground of the future. It's an obvious fact that parents have the responsibility to raise their children. They are your kids, so you feed them, clothe them, and see that they are educated. However, when we realize that through our children we can impact the world for Jesus Christ, it sheds a whole new light on it!

How many people when they grow up and experience life, talk about their Mom or Dad or Grandpa or Grandma? How many times have you heard someone talk about their praying Grandma? In the last NFL draft, one of the young superstars was celebrating with his Mom and Grandma. There were no men in the home - not unusual for this day in time. However the best man to have in the house is our heavenly Father. . and He's there for the asking

We call my wife Sherry "super nanny" because she pours her time, love, and energy into the two girls; not to mention she buys about half the baby clothes that sell on Ebay. Cody and Shandy's prayer and spiritual oversight is sending the girls down the unique path that God has for them. The girls God given gifts and talents are already being recognized and cultivated.

So, I'd like to salute my daughter Shandy and her husband Cody for taking their special ministry seriously; which is raising and training up Chloe and Heidi to be champions for the Lord. Congratulations champion Moms and Dads, Grandmas and Grandpas. Keep up the good work! Children can truly feel the love you give them and they will never be the same for it! Remember, you are sowing seeds of love into the ground of the future!

GO FOR IT!

Proverbs 22:6 *(nlt)* , *"Direct your children onto the right path; and when they are older, they will not leave it."*

Allison's Story

⸺∽⸺

*I*n the early eighties, I was having roping schools in the United States and Canada. One of my favorite schools was in Edgewood, New Mexico, east of Albuquerque. One of the students I worked with was a young promising champion named Todd Danley. Well, time flies and over twenty years later I get the privilege of helping coach his two daughters—Allison and Hayley. They are special young ladies that love the Lord and are dedicated to pursuing their rodeo dreams. Recently the girls competed at the American Junior Rodeo Association Finals in Glen Rose, Texas. Here's what happened in Allison's own words:

The 2011 AJRA Finals in Glen Rose was one of the best rodeo experiences of my life. I would like to thank the AJRA board for all their hard work in putting on a fantastic finals rodeo. Most importantly, thanks to God that I am still alive and able to write this. I had a great week competing and watching my friends. I went into the finals with a goal to win the All Around for the week in my age group. Winning the All Around would give me the chance to be one of the eight contestants given keys to the Dodge truck on Sunday. My strategy for the week was to go for third in every event; to make clean runs and catch all my cattle.

I ended up making it back to the short round in all my events: barrel racing, pole bending, goat tying, ribbon roping, breakaway roping, and with both partners in the team roping. Everything was going great until Saturday night at the short go. The first event was team roping, and I was up back to back with two different partners. My first run was with Megan Powell. I caught the steer by slick horns, but I was too close and the figure eight caught my horse's front feet. I dropped my rope, but it was too late. T.J. my 1.300 pound heading horse, tripped and rolled completely over the top of me. I felt something hit me in the chest, and saw his hooves inches from my face as he stopped rolling. I jumped up and away so I wouldn't get stepped on as he got up and was amazed to find that everything still worked.

After assuring very worried parents, judges, and team roping partners that I was completely fine, I jogged down the arena to get my horse. Thankfully, he wasn't hurt either and we were able to turn right around and make another run with Taylor Wharton, placing third in the round. The saying, "A setback is only the setup for a comeback," seems to apply to the rest of my night, which went well.

Long story short, I was one of the excited contestants standing on the stage on Sunday to draw a key that could possibly unlock a Dodge truck and the opportunity to drive it for a year! Words aren't able to describe how excited I was when my key unlocked the door!

As I look back on the week at the AJRA Finals, I like to think about the blessings God gave me. He protected me during the wreck, let me spend time with good friends, and on top of all that, I won the truck! I am reminded of my favorite Bible verse, **Jeremiah 29:11.** *"For I know the plans I have for you,"* declares the Lord, *"plans for good and not for evil, plans to prosper you, to give you hope and a future."*

Allison Danley

I love this story. Here is a hard-working champion that has a tough break-a potential disaster. However, the grace of God is with her—her life is spared. She gets back in the saddle again, gives her all and look what happens. How about you? Have you been through a wreck in your life? Have circumstances wrapped their cords around your feet and WHAM! Maybe you lost your marriage, your finances, your family, or your hope of a better life. There are people in your life that love God and are praying for you—ready to pick you up. Are you getting back up—are you looking for your horse? It's time to get back on. Isn't this story just like Jesus? **John 10:10** says *"the thief (Satan) comes to kill, steal and destroy —but I have come that you might have life and have it more abundantly."* What could have been the end of Allison's young life turned into her biggest moment.

That's exactly what God wants to do for you—prosper you and give you hope for the future. Great things can happen if you keep trusting and stay in the game. God has given you a key; the key to the abundant overcoming life on this earth, and the life to come. His name is Jesus, the key to everything you could ever hope for.

Jeremiah 29:11
I know the plans I have for you declares The Lord...

Allison (right) and the wreck

Plans
for
good...

Not
for
evil...

Plans
to prosper
you, to
give you
a hope
and a
future.

Champions Live Till They Leave

⊸⊷⊶⊷⊸

I was teaching a calf roping school in the mid-eighties between Edmonton and Calgary, Alberta. It was the first weekend of April and it was 30 degrees below zero - WOW! The good news is that we were in a heated indoor arena. We had taken a little break and I started visiting with one of the spectators in the grandstand. He told me he really enjoyed watching the calf roping school and wished that he wasn't too old to learn. I looked at this guy and thought to myself - Boy, he must be a lot older than he looks, because he didn't look that old. "How old are you?" I asked - He said, "I'm 29" and sighed as if he was about 107. I was amazed. "As a man thinks in his heart, so is he." (**Proverbs 23:7**)

In September 2004, a scene was unfolding that was a first in the rodeo world. The rodeo announcer at the Pendleton Round-up was introducing the next steer roper. If you are not acquainted with this rodeo event, the cowboy ropes the steer, jumps off his horse while the horse is still moving, and runs down to the steer that's lying on the ground and ties him up. This is a young man's sport, right? Or maybe not, because the next roper backing in the box is George Richmond from Hayden Lake, Idaho. He is 85 years young. He comes down the hill and hits the grass (football field) going nine-0, ropes the steer, lays his trip, gets off and ties him up. The crowd goes wild! Here's a word to live by, Champions live till they leave!

One of Satan's biggest tools is deception. He lies to people and tells them life is over for them. It's passed them by. It's too late to dream, to plan, and to be excited anymore. The chief question is, "Are you going to believe that?" If you do, then it's over. If you don't, your life has just begun! I was at a Walmart the other day and casually said to a stranger, "How are you today?" I was surprised as he answered sadly, "I'm just waiting around to die." I said, "Oh, don't do that! Live till you leave!"

How about the story of Joshua and Caleb. They were both 40 when the other 10 spies told the people the giants are too big and too overwhelming. Joshua and Caleb were ready then to take the land. For 40 years they had to wait till that entire unbelieving generation died. Listen to what Caleb says in **Joshua 14:10-14**, *"And now, behold, the Lord has kept me alive, as He said, these forty-five years since the Lord spoke this word to Moses, while the Israelites wandered in the wilderness: and now behold, I am this day eighty five years old. Yet I am as strong today as I was when Moses sent me; as my strength was then, so is my strength now for war and to go out and to come in. So now give me this hill country of which the Lord spoke that day. For you heard then how the (giant like) Anakim were there and that the cities were great and fortified; if the Lord will be with me, I shall drive them out just as the Lord said. Then Joshua blessed him and gave Hebron to Caleb son of Jephunneh for an inheritance. So Hebron became the inheritance of Caleb son of Jephunneh the Kenizzite to this day, because he wholly followed the Lord, the God of Israel."*

There you go champion - ask God for your mountain! He will help drive the giants from it. Someday, we're all going to a glorious place for eternity - meanwhile . . .

Champions Live Till They Leave

GO FOR IT!

George Richmond
Pendleton Round-up 2004

Dreams — F7

———— ∞∞∞ ————

*I*n the fall of 2007 I was about to go through major surgery. It is called hip resurfacing and it amounts to getting two new hip joints made out of titanium. The only surgery in my medical history was tonsil removal at the age of nine. I was a little concerned, and in much pain; however, looking forward to riding a horse again overrode the negatives. The day before I went in for pre-op testing, I had an interesting dream. In the dream I was at the Calgary Stampede rodeo with my good friend Phil Doan. Phil had a box of western shirts and was going to give me one. He asked me what size I wore. I told him either a large or an extra large. He answered me—"no you wear an F7." That was the end of the dream.

The next morning I told my wife Sherry the dream and we were contemplating what it meant. Sherry said. "We know that seven is God's number for completion." Then, as I was walking out to feed the horses, the Holy Spirit spoke in my heart; "Faith Completed." I knew exactly what He meant. We had been praying over this operation for over a year.... asking God to do His perfect work through the medical team that would operate on me.

The next day Sherry and I spent all day at Plaza Hospital going through tests and pre-op procedures. Now get this: Here's the last thing the main nurse told me, "After your surgery they will take you to the seventh floor—F7." Can you believe it? God gave me the dream to let me know in advance that He was with me, that our prayers had been answered, and that He knew the end from the beginning. My operation was a success.

Friend, what are you facing? Did you know God is not overwhelmed by it? **Psalm 118:6** tells us, *"The Lord is on my side of whom or what shall I fear."* Hebrews 13:5 (amp) says, *"God Himself has said, I will not in any way fail you nor give you up nor leave you without support. I will not, I will not, I will not in any degree leave you helpless, nor forsake you, nor let you down. Assuredly not!"*

I've got a box of western shirts—what size do you wear?

Medium, large or extra large? No friend, you wear an F7, that's a good shirt size for you—it's your perfect fit. <u>Faith Completed.</u> Trust Him. The victory is yours.

GO FOR IT!

Jeff roping on Sugar. Stephenville, Texas 1979

Closer Than You Think

⬧⬧⬧

I heard a story the other day about a man who had been working a gold mine for some time. He had been so sure there was gold there, but finally out of exhaustion and discouragement he gave up. The company he sold his mine to drilled a couple of inches deeper than he had gone and hit a giant gold strike!

About two years before I won the world championship, I got so tired of the financial pressure of pursuing my dream, that I almost threw in the towel and took a job in Walla Walla, Washington. Now it's one thing to stop and refuel your finances, but in this case it could have meant giving up on the dream especially when I was much closer than I thought. I'm so glad now that I didn't sell out. The gold buckle was closer than I knew!

Do you remember the Bible story in Genesis 25 about Isaac's son Esau? Esau came in from hunting one day, starved and exhausted. His brother Jacob was cooking some red stew. Esau said, "give me some of that red stew." Jacob replied, "All right, but trade me your blessing as the first born son." Esau said, "Look, I'm dying of starvation - what good is my birthright to me now?" So Esau gave up riches, favor, and blessing over one bowl of stew.

I want to encourage you champion - you're probably much closer than you think to your "break through and victory." In sports, in business, in your marriage, wherever, just one adjustment, one small change or just a little more time can make all the difference!

I had some roping schools in Australia in October of 2013. A talented young calf roper named Nate Eichorn went with me and did a great job helping me with the students. I made three small yet significant changes to his roping swing. 1. A little bit bigger loop. 2. Lifting the tip of his loop up to intersect the calf's shoulder. 3. Slowing the speed or tempo down slightly. These changes transformed him (in his words) from good to great. WOW!

Coaches and mentors can see one or two small things that can make all the difference. That's why they are so crucial to your success. They can not only help you but they can see that you are much closer than you think!

Has God put a dream in your heart? It's not time to consider quitting or backing off! It's time to move- move - move. Faith launches out - it's fearless - it doesn't hold back - it doesn't look back. We don't care what could have been - we're alive - we're living now - right now - today - no regrets. Have you got your headset on? Play some music that touches your heart - something that stirs up the champion in you.

Rock on champion. There's nothing impossible for you with the amazing God of Glory who is living in you! Don't miss the "gold" God has for your life. Drill a few inches more. Get a great mentor and stay with them. Don't sell out God's plan for your life for money, influence, fame, or temporary comfort. Many do and then grow old regretting what could have been. The dream He's put in your heart is closer, much closer than you think!

GO FOR IT!

Heb 10:35-37(amp), *"Do not, therefore fling away your fearless confidence, for it carries a great and glorious compensation of reward. For you have need of steadfast patience and endurance, so that you may perform and fully accomplish the will of God, and thus receive and carry away (and enjoy to the full) what is promised. For still a little while (a very little while), and the Coming One will come and He will not delay.*

Deb at the Omak Stampede

Champions Survive The Storm

~~~

In the fall of 1975, I was in hot pursuit of a world championship and had to fly into a coast town after dark in a small charter plane. Earlier the same year, I had a charter pilot run out of gas in both tanks between Roseburg and Portland, Oregon. After that experience, charter planes or charter pilots weren't exactly my idea of a good time. At first, I didn't understand why there were two pilots instead of the one that I had hired to fly me. It was dark when I got into the plane, and the second pilot was looking at a map with a fairly concerned look on his face.

We had flown for about an hour when we ran straight into a severe thunderstorm! Now, if you know anything about small airplanes and severe storms, the Apollo 13 phrase, "Houston, we have a problem," begins to take on a new meaning. We began to rock and roll as the lightning and rain attacked our small plane. Wow, every second seemed like an hour! At this point, one of the pilots commented that he wouldn't have tried to fly through this storm, but he knew how bad I needed to get to the rodeo.

Here's a tip: Always check your charter pilot's IQ level to see if it even registers on the graph. Little did they know that my life was more important to me than getting to that rodeo. Well, I survived that night by God's grace and mercy, but I'll never forget that storm.

Have you been going through a storm lately? Are your friends trying to pressure you into doing something that you know isn't right? You don't want to lose their friendship but you know this could turn into a bad storm. In **Matt. 7:24-27**, Jesus talks about the storm. He tells of two scenarios. The storm comes and blows on the first house, but because it is founded on rock, it stands. The same storm beats and blows on the second house, but because it was founded on sand, it was utterly destroyed. He explains the house founded on rock was the person who hears the word of God and does it. The house on sand is the person who knows God's word and doesn't do it.

Do you remember the story of Jesus and his disciples on the sea when the bad storm came? The disciples panicked; yet, Jesus was asleep. They woke him up and said, "Don't you care that we're about to die?" Then Jesus rebuked the storm, and it was totally calm. He said, "Why are you so fearful? Don't you have faith?"

Storms can be all kinds - marital, physical, financial, family or whatever. Is your house built on the rock? Remember the three pigs? Only one was prepared for the coming (wolf) destruction. You may be going through a storm right now, or you may be experiencing nothing but blue skies.

However, let me give you a friendly warning: "storms come to everyone." Here are four keys to encourage you through your storm:

1. If you're a Christian, Jesus is in the boat and He will not jump ship on you. If you're not a Christian - great time to give your life to Him!

2. Stay Cool! Fear, panic, anxiety, worry, dread and torment aren't going to help you. They will only worsen whatever you're going through.

3. **Romans 8:28** is truly an amazing scripture - it says: ..."*all things work together for good to those who love God...*" Think about it, whatever you've been going through - good, bad or ugly - Jesus has promised (He's guaranteeing you) it's all going to work for your good! Our part is simply to believe it.

4. In the midst of the storm - begin to praise Him. Scripture says in **Ps.22:2** that "*He inhabits the praise of His people.*" Plus: praise stills the avenger. " It zips the devils lips."

So you're in a storm champion! Here's the good news - you and your great God (your eternal best friend) are going to overcome it! God doesn't want the storms of life to destroy you, Go

to His Word - to His refuge; He will always see you through!
- Remember -

CHAMPIONS SURVIVE THE STORM

Psalm 25:5 *(nlt), "Lead me by your truth and teach me, for you are the God who saves me. All day long I put my hope in you."*

Foot Race

—◆◆◆—

I was in Billings, Montana a few years ago, and met up with my dad there. I flew in from Texas and he came from Washington. We spoke at a church in Hardin, Montana; and just had an awesome time with our friends Mark and Shelley Cain, and Tim and Colleen Moulette. While I was there I got to see Nate Eichorn - a tough young calf roper who had come to my roping school a few years earlier. We were busy doing a lot of things; but I wanted to see him rope some calves before we flew home.

So before the weekend was over, we got to squeeze a few hours in. I made a couple of suggestions and his roping literally skyrocketed. WOW! He was excited and so was I. I invited him to come to Texas for coaching and he said , "I'm coming!" However, before he could get to Texas, I told him I was going on a cowboy mission trip to Australia. I asked him if he would like to come with me and help me teach roping schools and speak at churches. Well, He was up for the adventure. I was pleasantly surprised and impressed that this young cowboy was game and gutsy.

It was October of 2013 and off we went. Nate flew from Bozeman, Montana to Los Angeles - then to Sydney and onto Brisbane, Australia. I flew non-stop from Dallas/ Ft. Worth to Brisbane. Nate and I stayed with our friends David and Lynn Boske. We enjoyed some great sleep and fellowship for the first two days.

We had our first school in Caboolture, Queensland. Nate tied down about 20 big fresh calves preparing for the school. Some of them were big, wild and strong. I gained a new respect for him. He was a little bit bruised, battered and weary; but he did it! We had a great time there with our friends Peter and Kathy Boske; and then off we went to Warwick, Queensland to do another school.

We had several girl breakaway ropers that I nick-named the "no misses." One morning we had cowboy church before we started roping. I had never seen anything quite like it! Toward the end of the service, almost everyone was weeping. It was something special. We began to pray for one person after another. We had a great time in the Lord! Then out to the arena we went!

I was working with one group while Nate had his own students. Then someone hollered, "Hey, we've got a foot race over here!" By the time I turned around, Nate and Bonnie were "flying" across the arena. Nate got to the end of the arena first, but not by much. Then after a short rest, they "smoked" across the arena again! That night the two foot racers went to eat Chinese food. How does the saying go? "The rest is History!" They fell in love! A Montana cowboy and an Australian cowgirl. Bonnie is the daughter of our special Aussie friends Alan and Roz Flood. Alan is an Australian champion calf roper.

Fast forward to April 2015 - Kilarney, Queensland - it's time for the wedding! WOW! Jesus said in Matthew 6:33 (nkjv), "But seek first the kingdom of God and His righteousness, and all these things shall be added to you." What was amazing, is that Nate was not looking for a lady at all; but God knew more than Nate. I believe Nate was truly putting God's kingdom first as he worked alongside me.

Three things impacted me about this young champion: (1) Nate flew there at his own expense, (2) he worked so hard to help the ropers in Australia, and (3) he had the courage to get out of his comfort Zone. Life is an incredible, awesome adventure when we put Jesus first. He is real! He is wonderful! He has a match made in heaven for you! He has blessings for you that are more wonderful than you can even think, dream or imagine!

Nate and Bonnie Eichorn with Nash

Maybe you need to launch out and begin a new journey in your life putting God first. OK Runners - on your mark - get set - Go!

God wants you to win!

P.S. UPDATE: Nate and Bonnie have a beautiful baby boy named Nash. Now the three of them are running their race to win! God is Good!

Lamar Colorado

I was rodeoing in the 80's and on my way to a rodeo in Lamar, Colorado. Before I left Casper, Wyoming, world champion Dave Brock told me about this crazy calf that was in the draw at Lamar. He was calf #34, and everyone who had drawn him had gotten the whistle. That means they couldn't tie him in under 35 seconds. Well, I got to Lamar that night and guess what? I drew that tiger-striped crazy calf #34. Not good! Well, here's what happened.

I was one of the last ropers during the performance that night, and one of the first ropers was hall of famer Roy Cooper. I don't remember exactly how it happened, but Roy got in a roping wreck and was hurt. He rode back to the bull doggin box and slid off his horse and someone caught him. Before I could even think about it, I was off of my horse and praying for him. I prayed for a while, and finally Roy looked up at me and said, "They're calling your name, you need to rope." I got on my horse and proceeded to chase one bad calf. One of the rodeo clowns was helping pull the barrier and said later that I should have broken the barrier by 4 feet. He couldn't believe it was still tied together. I roped the calf in 3 swings, and when I got half way down the rope, (instead of running at me like he had done with every one else), old tiger-stripe just stood there, staring at me. I ran right on into him, flanked and tied him in 9.3 seconds, winning the rodeo. Hold it—this can't be the same monstrous calf that Dave had told me about...but it sure was!

I could hardly believe it, and neither could the calf ropers that knew how bad this calf was. I believe with all my heart that this was a **Matthew 6:33** story. Jesus said if we would put the kingdom of God first, He would add the earthly things to us that we need. Earthly things like winning a rodeo. Because I was more concerned about praying for Roy than I was about competing at the rodeo, the Holy Spirit supernaturally intervened. He showed me and others that He can do amazing things in any impossible situation. He can bless us when all circumstances oppose us.

Let me clarify something. Is this some kind of a gimmick to let you win? Do Christians get special favor in order to win? For the most part, my answer would be "No." However there are times when God will show Himself in an awesome, real way as He did at Lamar that night. Here's a tip—we've come to the rodeo to win and we've got to be focused to win. However, sometimes we need to remind ourselves that our whole purpose on this earth is to bring the love of God to others. Put Jesus first in your life and watch Him do the impossible.

GO FOR IT!

Matt 6:33 *(nlt),* " *Seek the Kingdom of God above all else, and live righteously, and He will give you everything you need."*

Cow Palace in San Francisco, California 1973

H.I.T.

*I*t was the mid 1980's and I was in Canada with my friend Hayseed Stephens. Hayseed was a former quarterback with the New York Jets; and was now successful in the oil business. He was there to negotiate an oil lease. One night I had a dream. In the dream I saw an arrow with three letters - H.I.T. (See picture) The letters stood for Honesty, Integrity and Truth.

Then a voice in the dream said, "the people that Hayseed is negotiating with are laying a trap for him. They are going to rob him if he signs a contract with them." Well, I told Hayseed the dream and he withdrew all offers as graciously as he could. Within two days he found out what the group had planned. It was a trap and it would have bankrupted him. He was so thankful that the Holy Spirit gave me that dream. The arrow of Honesty, Integrity and Truth had hit the bulls eye on greed, lies, and corruption.

It was 1919 and the Chicago White Sox and Cincinnati Reds were "squaring off" in the world series. Something unparalleled happened that year. Crooked gamblers contacted several White Sox players to fraudulently "fix" the game. The series played out and sure enough Chicago lost. Before it was over, eight players were banned from baseball for life and the integrity of America's favorite past time was marred for decades. Webster's dictionary defines "fraud" as wrongful or criminal deception intended to result in financial or personal gain.

It was the 1980's and a special friend of mine (an NFR calf roper) decided to go into politics. Well-liked and respected, he was voted County Commissioner. Get this - several years later, my friend and very few other commissioners in his state were the only ones that didn't go to prison for taking bribes from companies selling them county road equipment, etc. He refused to compromise what was right! Since then God has richly blessed him!

One time the Lord spoke in the heart of a friend of mine. He said, "son, the only things I want to take from your life are the things that could kill you or bring devastation to your life." Bribes, fraud, under the table dealings usually come in attractive packages. They come under the guise that there is no harm done. "What's the big deal.?" The big deal is that when you sell out your personal honesty and integrity and truth for money; you minimize the value that your life has; plus it opens the door for shame, punishment and destruction!

Hey champion! If someone or some life situation comes slithering into your life to get you to sell out, to compromise what you know is right - rebuke that thing in Jesus' name and then get away from it. Distance yourself suddenly before that snake bites you. Champions, we are his polished arrows to shoot His message of honesty, integrity and truth into the world!

GO FOR IT!

Proverbs 1:8 *(message)*, *"Nobody robs a bank with everyone watching. Yet that's what these people are doing - they're doing themselves in. When you grab all you can get, that's what happens; the more you get, the less you are."*

Proverbs 11:3 *(ASV)*, *"The integrity of the upright shall guide them; But the perverseness of the treacherous shall destroy them.*

Overcoming Rejection

I can still remember being in the third grade in Post Falls, Idaho. Most of the time at recess we would run to the playground and play football. But before we could start, we had to choose teams. The daily ritual was whoever was the first to say "second captain first choice" got to choose the first player. Then the other captain chose and so on until everyone was selected. Now, this may sound fairly harmless, but it became real sticky at the end. The last players were chosen hesitatingly by the captains - almost a "well if I have to, I'll choose you" attitude. At the time I'm sure none of us realized the lifelong issues that were being developed.

Are there many things in life more demeaning or degrading than your peers not choosing you or wanting you? Being rejected by your friends is a hard pill to swallow. The good news was, once the game began, no one thought about it until the next day and we chose again. I loved football from the time I was about five years old; as a result I never personally experienced rejection at the recess games. However, years later I would know exactly how some of the third grade boys felt. It was 1978, after much searching, Sherry and I came to a conclusion - we are giving our lives to Jesus Christ. Well, we did and everything changed. Yes, everything! We knew something radical and wonderful had changed us; we were on cloud nine!

But what about my "third graders" - I mean my rodeo buddies? Well, they didn't know what to think of the new Jeff. I wasn't going to the bars with them, wasn't telling lewd jokes or listening to them, and I wasn't using the same x-rated language, etc. My friends began to stay away in droves. Before the rodeo as we were exercising our horses in the main arena; it seemed like I was always riding alone. This verse took on new meaning to me: **II Cor. 5:17** – *"Therefore if any man be in Christ, he is a new creature, old things are passed away, behold all things are become new."*

Then get this: I was rodeoing in Medicine Hat, Alberta; and someone asked me if I would give my testimony at the Sunday morning rodeo church service. I said "yes," but little did I know that the people organizing the service would put "Jeff Copenhaver Preaching this Sunday" posters all around the rodeo arena. I wasn't preaching; I was just giving my testimony. Yet in the eyes of my peers, I had become a preaching evangelist. It may have intimidated me at first; but I realized later that this was probably the best thing that ever happened to me. Jesus said in Luke 10:16, "If they rejected me, they will reject you." We need to ride alone if necessary.

So many Christians slip and slide around their families, friends, work buddies, etc, afraid to really let the 'cat out of the bag' that they have given their lives to Jesus. Jesus said in **Matt 10:32, "If you confess me before men, I will confess you before the Father, and if you deny me before men, I will deny you before the Father."** So, for a season most of my peers stayed away, but the story wasn't over. As time went on my friends found out that what had happened to me was real. I prayed for my friends and many of them became Christians!

Are you afraid of rejection? Do you think it would be the end of the world if your friends left you and made fun of you? Yes, it would hurt for a little while, but at the same time something even greater would be happening in you. You would be growing spiritually, and becoming God's special set-apart champion.

The truth is, your friends are looking for something that is real and life changing. As you are willing to stand alone if necessary for a season; they will see Jesus in you. Your light may be the only light they will ever see.

GO FOR IT!!

Crazy Connections

◆━━━◆◆◆━━━◆

*I*n the summer of 1975 the race for the calf roping championship was hot and heavy. I liked the rodeos in the northwest the best because the cattle were more even and less of a drawing contest. Being raised in the northwest, I knew the ropers there and which of their horses I felt I could win on the best.

My challenge, or predicament was how to work Longview, Washington and Hillsboro, Oregon in the same night. One rodeo started at 7:30 P.M. and the other started at 8:00 P.M. They were approximately 70 miles apart. For all intents and purposes this was an impossibility. Well, here's what happened.

Longview, Washington had a helicopter ride that operated with the carnival on the grounds. I roped my calf at Longview, jumped over the arena fence and got into the helicopter that was already cranked up and ready. He took me to the Longview airport just a few minutes away. The plane there was running and took off immediately after I got in. We flew as fast as we could to Hillsboro, Oregon where a car was waiting to take me to the rodeo grounds.

When I ran into the arena the fifth roper was roping, and I was the eighth roper - pretty close, huh? I made a pretty good run and tied my calf fast enough to win what I guessed to be about third place. But the secretary announced, "I'm sorry, I missed your time - you'll have to run him again after the rodeo." I didn't know if I should be devastated or encouraged. However I roped the calf again after the rodeo, made a better run and won first place. I was really pumped!

When you do the impossible, God is truly glorified. The question is not "Can we do this," it's "how are we going to do it?" In the book of Luke, an angel appeared to Zacharias and told him that his barren wife was going to have a son that would do great things for God. Zach's reply displeased God because it was a loser's response. He asked God, and I paraphrase, "How can I know this will really happen?" The spirit behind his seemingly innocent question was "I don't believe you." (pure doubt and unbelief)

In the same chapter, an angel comes to Mary, who was a virgin, and tells her she will have a child without being intimate with a man. Mary said, "How is this going to happen?" God told her, and then she said (paraphrased) "According to Your Word, God let it be done." The spirit behind Mary's questions was: not if, but how. It is so exciting to do what everyone tells you is impossible to do. "All things are possible to him that believes." (**Mark 9:23**)

One of the Hebrew names for God is Elohim. It means God, our Creator. The creative God of the universe lives inside you. When you are moved by faith, nothing is impossible to you. When you ask God "how are we going to get this done?" Get ready. Ask God how, and He will show you. The glorious, creative God of the universe will bring His creative thoughts to your mind. The impossible becomes possible!

GO FOR IT!

Luke 1:37 (*Jubilee bible 2000*), *"For with God nothing is impossible."*

Jeff flying in helicopter to airplane in Longview, Washington

Salt Lake City

—⊸⧫⧫⧫⊷—

By Sherry Copenhaver

Life was going great as God had been the center of it for several months now. Jeff and I had given our hearts to Jesus in Ft. Worth, Texas and then had gotten baptized with the power of the Holy Spirit. (a very real second experience after salvation that gives you the power to witness and live an overcoming life. - Acts 2:4) Our journey of adventure had begun with God, and He had become so real and amazing to us that we were beside ourselves. One of the things that became apparent was that the Lord wanted to heal and deliver us from some of the negative things of our past.

From the time I was a little girl, I could count on both hands, all the things I was afraid of. Some of which were: fear of staying alone when we were small (sometimes my parents had to go to the city for a day - I was 12 years old); fear of storms, fear of accidents, fear of being attacked by someone, fear of public speaking, fear of heights and especially fear of death and not knowing for sure if I would go to heaven. These are tormenting lies sent from the enemy to hold us captive. (John 10:10) However, there are many promises in the Bible that say that Jesus will deliver us from all our fears.

You know God will not leave you hopeless in the same state He found you in. I think some Christians don't know that because they are always trying to duck out of God's will for them; they have a fear of change! We can trust God with our very lives and He loves us so much that He wants to break these demonic strongholds and set us free to enjoy His abundant life. One of these strongholds is fear.

Remember I said I had a fear of staying alone and being attacked. Well, about a year into our walk with God, a situation happened in Salt Lake City that brought me to a closer trust in the Lord's protection.

Jeff and I were rodeoing and he had to fly from Salt Lake

City (where we were) to Pendleton, Oregon. I was to spend the night there with the horses and meet him the next day (8 hours later) in Oregon. I was driving the truck with horses and trailer. The plan was that I would spend the night alone at the rodeo grounds. There was a high fence enclosure (with two-strand barb wire on top) around the whole area with a big gate that the security guard kept locked. So we felt like it was a particularly safe spot. When evening came, I realized I was the only camper left in there. I was parked close to the barns, where the horses were; and did I mention the guard dogs in a stall nearby? About 10:30 PM after checking horses, and locking the camper, I settled in(thinking all was well) for the night.

It was not a matter of about 10 minutes when the dogs started sounding off. Until then everything had been quiet. So thinking some critter was snooping around, I settled back down under the covers. Suddenly I felt the camper shaking; it was a "cab over camper" on the back of our truck (popular in the 80's). Then it shook again! My heart sickened and fear gripped every part of my being. I looked back toward the locked door and saw the latch being turned.

Then I saw the shadow of a person pass by the lower camper window. My first thought was this cannot be happening to me. I'm all alone, no Jeff, no gun, no security guard (he had left at 10:00 and locked the gate behind him) - so there was no way out. Then I remembered, we had been reading and studying God's Word faithfully for the last couple of years and after a split second of these "fear thoughts" - this rose up in my spirit: "You have angels, the blood of Jesus and a promise of protection in Psalm 91" Wow!! I asked God to send a giant guardian angel to help me; and I said: " the blood of Jesus is around me and this camper.". I said that about 10 times and quoted what I did know of Psalm 91.

Within minutes of this (seemed like hours) there was the noisiest banging, clanging and commotion outside that was so loud, I clamored to the other end of the bed to look out the window. Since there were large lights outside by the fence, I saw two shadowy figures scrambling up that 10 foot fence (as if they were on fire) and over the top to the outside. It looked like a giant gorilla was chasing them. Wow! I knew it was my angel!! Maybe one day in heaven, I will get to see a replay of what happened. No one else was in those grounds that night but me, guard dogs locked in a stall, security guard gone with the gate locked.

Supernatural! - Yes. God's promises working!! Yes. Authority over the situation!! Yes. Deliverance from my fears! Yes. God in control!! Yes. Can I trust Jesus with my life?!! Yes. Does He love and protect us if we call upon Him?! Yes. This was a real turning point in my life; and it will always be etched in my spirit as to the power of His name! Thanks be to God. Trusting and speaking His word worked for me. If it worked for me - it will work for you. Only dare to believe and trust in Him and His goodness.

By the way I did make it to the rodeo on time, Jeff won some money and I had a marvelous testimony.

Psalm 34:4 (niv), *"I sought the Lord, and he answered me; he delivered me from all my fears.*

Palm 91:5-6 (niv),*"You will not fear the terror of night, nor the arrow that flies by day nor the pestilence that stalks in the darkness, nor the plague that destroys at midday."*

Sherry and Sugar

Success is Not What You Accomplish
It's What You Overcome

Have you ever had a day when everything seemed to go really wrong? I'm talking about the kind of day where you're tempted to get back into bed, go to sleep, wake up and try it all over again? Well, I had a day like that recently. Physically I was in pain, financially I had a challenge and when I rode my favorite horse, he acted like his good horse sense had gone on vacation. I finally made it through the day slightly battered; and when evening came I was ready for a peaceful nights sleep.

That night I had a dream, and in the dream the Lord spoke so clearly to me. He said: "Success is not what you accomplish, it's what you overcome!" WOW! Ten words from heaven – ten words that I really needed. The next morning as I began to dress, everything in my attitude, perspective and overall outlook had changed! I realized with such clarity that the prize isn't necessarily the end accomplishment, but in overcoming whatever needs to be dealt with that day. I also knew that if I was going to overcome, it would be done in God's power. Look at **I John 5:4.** *"For whatever is born of God overcomes the world; and this is the victory that overcomes the world, even our faith".*

Our faith in Him is what overcomes—our faith in His promises. That next morning I purposed to lock in on God's promise in every area of my life. Well, get this—within 5 days my physical pain left, my financial situation turned around, my horse did better than ever, and two or three other things got better. **Psalm 34:19** says, *"Many are the afflictions of the righteous, but the Lord delivers him from them all."* Jesus didn't say we wouldn't have challenges, but He did say we could overcome and be victorious if we would seek Him and walk in the power of His Word. What are you dealing with today,—relationally, maritally, financially, or physically? Has discouragement, worry, confusion, self pity

Deb exiting right—even the best have bad days.

or shame come to steal your joy, your peace, your excitement or hope for living? Are your friends at school making fun of you or giving you a bad time? Do your dreams appear so faint that they feel like they're in another galaxy? Well, let me encourage you—success is not what you accomplish, it's what you overcome.

The year I won the calf roping championship was the toughest year of my life. As I was in pursuit of my life dream, I experienced some incredible obstacles—financial hardships, physical exhaustion, and extreme disappointment. One at a time I had to deal with them and decide whether or not I would continue forward. My success that year was truly not the gold belt buckle, but the choice of continuing forward—not folding under the storms of difficulty.

Let's put faces with stories on overcoming. My wife, Sherry found this on the internet; a thalidomide baby girl born with no arms is now grown up and is an accomplished horse woman. She rides with her reins in her mouth, and she bridles her horse with her feet. She competes in Olympic dressage. Incredible—she overcomes! A young pianist from China is the best of the best! He plays beautiful classical music with his feet, because he has no arms. A college wrestler wins almost all of his matches. Does he have anything to overcome? No legs; yes you heard me right. And there is the man who has no arms or legs and drives his own car and loves to swim? Now we can see why true success (or winning) is not what you accomplish, it's what you overcome. These people are overcomers—champions at the highest level. Everyone in life is dealt a different hand. We have to play the cards we have, and with Him we can...overcome!

1 John 5:4 *(amp), "For whatever is born of God is victorious over the world, and this is the victory that conquers the world, even our faith."*

Champions Seek Perfection

$\mathcal{J}$ backed into the roping box at the Cow Palace in San Francisco. It was the first time I had qualified for the finals at a major rodeo. Unfortunately, I blew it. I took a bad throw and missed. I let the pressure of the moment shift my focus to the crowd rather than the task at hand. Before I had ridden out of the arena, I realized the spectators could care less if I did good or bad that night. They were looking to the next roper, period.

It was a tough lesson but I purposed in my heart after that night that I wouldn't let the crowd or what others were thinking distract my focus again. Champions learn from mistakes and know they are not final. They realize they learn more from their failures than their successes. The hardest lessons stay with us the longest and remain the deepest. All around rodeo champion Ty Murray made a great statement that was obviously something he lived by. He said, "I either win something or I learn something." Sounds like win – win, doesn't it? In life, we can either win or learn something. We can purpose to learn from our mistakes, or put the blame on someone or something else. That leads to a life of excuses – a loser's road. Ty used this principal and attitude to become one of rodeo's all-time greats. You can use this principle to become a champion in or out of the arena.

Champions are always pushing, practicing and pressing for perfection!

Champions never look at life as "well, that's good enough". Something in them shoots for perfection. Good is not good enough! Great is the goal. Working at their dream is never work; it's pure joy! Picture an ice skater up every day before daylight skating and skating and skating. A boxer trains for months and months, preparing for the fight that could test his strength, endurance and courage to the limit. Every hour, every thought, every dollar spent, every ounce of effort gets him one precious step closer. Champions love to practice; perhaps they have a more simplistic approach to life – find one thing and get really good at it!

How about your life? The apostle Paul said in **Phil. 3:13-14**, *"I press on toward the goal to win the supreme and heavenly prize to which God in Christ Jesus is calling us upward."* Paul would let nothing stop the process of perfection that God was working in his life. Paul knew that God, in His process of perfection, was working all things together for good for his life and his destiny. He knew the adventure he was on was a journey of perfection – to God's glory. Is that your outlook? Are you willing to let go of the hurt, the disappointment, the embarrassment and let God perfect you so that He can use you on this earth to His glory?

When you become born again, the Holy Spirit begins His adventure of perfection in you. He is the potter; we are the clay. He will shape you into His champion! Don't settle for less. Go for all that you were created for. I encourage you champion - you're heading for perfection.

GO FOR IT!

Deb Copenhaver and Casey Tibbs
behind the chutes at Madison Square Garden

Five Card Stud

For probably 10 to 15 years after I became a Christian, I knew I would write a poem called "Five Card Stud." Well one day the Holy Spirit began to give me these words and here it is:

This was the biggest card game that the world had ever seen! The game was down to two players, satan, the prince of darkness and Jesus Christ, the King of Kings. The stakes were high for all men's souls. Would man suffer torment or walk on streets of gold? "Deal'em," satan spoke from a guttural throat. "It'll be no time now and I'll collect my note." "Five card stud's the game!" the dealer proclaims, "Ante up boys!"

The game begins, each player gets his first card; it's buried face down; it's called your "hole card" and it's what the game revolves around. The devil's second card is an Ace of Spades, the death card leads the way. Jesus gets a King of Hearts. . . His life was on display. Then the third card came, another Ace to satan; he cries "This game is mine!" Jesus gets another King, silent, trusting the divine. The pressure builds, all eternity tenses. Will mankind go free or be shut in wiry fences? The dealer rolls the fourth card to slewfoot, a Jezebel Queen. Jesus gets a 3 of Hearts, no help. "My God, My God, why have you forsaken me!?" There is blood flowing down Jesus' back as the last card is dealt, the sky is black in the middle of the day, "It is finished!" he yelled. Jesus gets a two of Hearts, again, "No help!"

Now picture this:

With the cards all out, 4-up and 1-down, satan has a pair of Aces showing. He looks at his "hole card" and frowns. Then with a gleam of arrogance, he pushes all his chips in the middle and tells Jesus, "Sonny boy, you're goin' down!" Then with all the power of the universe, Jesus calmly takes His stand, He calls the bet, then shows his 5-card hand. He rolls a king - 3 Kings for royalty, 3 Kings for the Trinity, 3 Kings for you and me. Well, all creation waited and looked over to the other side to see if satan really had the goods or if he only lied.

Now let me tell you some Good News about the One who set you free. If you know Jesus as your Savior, you'll be shoutin' and dancin' for eternity. Meanwhile, back to the card game; I want you to take this one to the bank. When Jesus shed His blood at Calvary,

HE MADE THE DEVIL'S "HOLE CARD" BLANK!

What does it mean to you personally that the devil's hole card is blank? Everything! If you have received Jesus as your Savior and confessed Him to others (Romans 10:9-10) then the devil has no power over you. He can't continue to steal from you. **Hebrews 2:14**, *"...that through death he might destroy him that had the power of death, that is, the devil."* If you are born again, God has dealt you the winning hand! Having the winning hand alone is not enough. You have to call the devil's bluff when he tells you you're going to die, go bankrupt, lose your wife, family, or whatever. When he slides all his greasy chips out into the middle of the table of your life and cackles; you're going to need the Word of God in your heart to combat him . You'll have to call his bluff with your own pile of chips, which are God's Words.

Read and study Matthew 4 where satan tempted Jesus. Jesus kept calling his bluff with "it is written..." So can you! **James 4:7**, *"Submit yourselves to God, resist the devil and he will flee from you!"* Don't forget the devil's "hole card" is blank; but you still have to call his bluff! Standing on God's word will bring the victory for you! My dad before he was saved, loved to play poker. After he received Jesus, he told me- "this is the best gamble I've ever made!" I said, you're right - because it's no gamble at all!"

GO FOR IT!

Fort Worth, Texas — 1974

It was the early 70's and a good friend of mine, Warren Wuthier, gave me one of the best rodeo tips I've ever had. He told me, "Jeff, when you go to the big rodeos that have a short go or finals, never quit hustling. Even if it looks like your calf is no good or you've gone too far down the arena, hustle to the max to the last tenth of a second. The reason for this is the big rodeos usually take twelve contestants to the finals, and if you can get in the top twelve, anything can happen. A lot of finals tend to fall apart." By the way, Warren was a runner up PRCA All Around Champion and a NFR Steer Wrestler, and tie down qualifier - a good person to take advice from. So from then on especially at Denver, Houston, Ft. Worth, San Antonio, Cheyenne, Pendleton, Calgary, and others, I would hustle to the very max. When I finished a run and threw my hands up, I was satisfied that I couldn't have been one tenth of a second faster.

In 1974 I was roping at Ft. Worth, Texas, which was - two head and a finals. I didn't draw too good on my first two calves, but I never quit trying. I slipped into the finals in eleventh place. I remembered what Warren told me "anything can happen." Well, it did. We were roping real big calves, and I was the second roper in reverse order. I tied my calf in 10.0 seconds flat. Now there were ten ropers left. One by one they either missed, broke a barrier, or their calf got up. One roper's plane was delayed so he got there too late! I won first. Can you believe it? Warren was right.

How many times in life do we just go through the motions and yet we think we're doing our best? It's easy to get in a rut and take life for granted. Until Warren gave me that tip, I didn't realize that I was unconsciously letting up. Letting up is just another way to say "giving up." Jesus said, "in this world you will have tribulation,--." We can't afford to let up in any area of our lives. Whether it comes against your dream, your marriage, your business or your walk with God – it's all the same. Tribulation comes in the form of disappointment and discouragement to take the air right out of your sails. Don't fall for it! Why? Because, after Jesus said, "In this world you'll have tribulation," He said, "but be of good cheer for I have overcome the world." He's already overcome for us. Isn't that awesome? That's why we're not letting up. One time the Lord spoke in my heart –"if you'll give it all you've got, I'll show you all I've got!"

GO FOR IT!

Colossians 3:23 *(message), " Don't just do the minimum that will get you by. Do your best. Work from the heart for your real MASTER, for God."*

Our special friends,
The Danley Family, Todd, Allison , Hayley, and Jerre

World's Richest Roping

⊰⊱

t was 1977 and a lot of things were changing in my life. Winning a world championship in 1975 was the fulfillment of a life-long dream. However, on the down side, it fell way short of being what I expected. I had made rodeo my whole life and my god. This began a search in my life for something more. I met my wife Sherry at the Calgary Stampede rodeo in 1976. She had been married to a millionaire and was looking for something more than money and a jet-set lifestyle.

I rodeoed enough to qualify for the NFR (National Finals Rodeo) in 1976. However, my heart was definitely not in rodeo. I sold my good horse Streak in 1977 and took the year off. That was a "God thing" for me. I found out that there is life outside of rodeo.

In the fall of 1977 I began to rope some and was making plans to compete at Clem Mc Spadden's "World's Richest Roping." This was a $1000 entry fee roping - biggest in the country. Two days before the roping, I bought a new horse named Sugar. I named him that because he was sweet. He and I had great timing together from the very beginning! But here's the deal! Sugar was in pretty rough shape physically. Kind of skinny, rough haired and needed new shoes. I told Sherry we only have a one horse trailer, so we're just taking my friend Bob Bristol's horse. Sherry's response was, "We need to take Sugar - we'll borrow a two-horse trailer." I responded with "No, he's not ready." Fortunately I lost the argument to a smart lady. We borrowed a two-horse trailer, loaded up Sugar and headed for Oklahoma.

We got to Bushyhead and found out that the average weight of the calves we were roping was 333 lbs. They were big calves and could they ever run! The score or (head start) was long and I barely caught my first two calves at the very end of the arena. Sherry met me at the gate as I was riding out of the arena. I looked at her and said, "I know, it's time to switch horses and ride Sugar." I love my lady. Hey guys, do you listen to your better half?

Sugar didn't look great, but he worked "out of this world."

Plus, he was incredibly fast. I made six more runs (an 8-header) and roped as good as I had roped in my whole life. Sugar and I were an instant team. I won the roping and $14,500. A new single event payoff record at that time. I had a new respect and appreciation for Sherry and had paid for Sugar ($5000) plus almost $10,000 more.

But get this; as Sherry and I were leaving town, I began to cry. She said, "What's the matter?" I said, "I don't know how to explain it, but I had some help out there today. It was like the Lord was riding with me - I could feel His presence!" Now remember, Sherry and I had been on a God search for about two years. **Romans 2:4** says, *"His kindness is intended to turn you from your sins."* God is so personal that He revealed Himself to me cowboy style at the biggest calf roping in the world. He knew what it took to convince a calf roper. Seven months later Sherry and I knelt down at the foot of our bed and asked Jesus Christ to come into our hearts.

Let me ask you a question: Are you on a God search? Are you wondering if He's real? If you are, I can guarantee you He will show Himself real to you in a personal way. As you begin to realize His incredible love for you, it will cause your heart to open to Him like mine did. You can ask the Lord - are you real?- do you love me? - do you have a special plan for my life? - Is my life significant? He will answer you and reveal Himself to you in an awesome way.

If you're already a born again believer, you need to continue that search to know Him better and better; and realize the incredible life He has for you! Riding Sugar that day was sweet - feeling the Lord's presence with me that day was mega-sweet! He's awesome!!

GO FOR IT!

Psalms 34:8 *(amp), "O taste and see that the Lord (our God) is good! Blessed (happy, fortunate, to be envied) is the man who trusts and takes refuge in Him."*

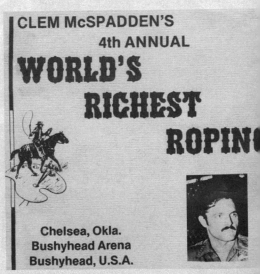

CLEM McSPADDEN'S
4th ANNUAL
WORLD'S RICHEST ROPING

Chelsea, Okla.
Bushyhead Arena
Bushyhead, U.S.A.

Overcoming Humiliation

———— ∞∞∞ ————

*I*t was October 1975, and there was only a handful of rodeos left before the National Finals. I was barely in the lead for the world championship in the calf roping which caused every calf to take on the importance of a fourth quarter play in the Super Bowl. The rodeo was Dallas, Texas with over 100 of the toughest calf ropers in the country entered. We were all roping our first of two calves the day before the actual rodeo performances started.

I borrowed a horse from a friend, because I had left my good horse, Streak, at the Portland, Oregon rodeo. Portland was being held on the same week end as Dallas. Riding borrowed horses was not my favorite thing, but there is no choice when you're competing at several rodeos at the same time. I backed into the box knowing it was time to rope my best. I roped my calf really quick, but as I was getting off, my right foot slipped out of the stirrup. I hit the ground like a high diver doing a belly flop. I got up, a little stunned, got my bearings and then flanked and tied my calf.

It was bad enough not to win anything, but to be humiliated like that in front of all my peers was hard to swallow. I flew to Portland that night knowing I must put the disappointment and humiliation of Dallas behind me immediately. I won both go-rounds and the average at Portland. It was probably the most crucial win of the whole year. I gave Streak a big kiss! I had gone from experiencing the lowest low to the highest high.

Have you ever been humiliated? Webster's dictionary defines the word humiliate, "to reduce to a lower position in one's own estimation or the estimation of others." Humiliation in one form or another happens to all of us. Sometimes it's our fault, and sometimes it's a product of life's circumstances.

One of the great champions in history was the Apostle Paul,

who wrote a big percentage of the New Testament and went through a long list of humiliations. He was stoned, whipped, beat with rods, shipwrecked, snake bitten, misunderstood by Christians and non-Christians alike; yet Paul had a secret weapon that always took him from defeat to victory.

What was it? **Phil. 3:13-14** (Living Bible), *"No, Dear brothers, I am still not all I should be but I am bringing all my energies to bear on this one thing - forgetting the past and looking forward to what lies ahead. I strain to reach the end of the race and receive the prize for which God is calling us up to heaven because of what Christ Jesus did for us."*

Some of you have been humiliated through divorce, losing your family, bankruptcy, being sent to prison, broken dreams, etc. It may have been your fault or someone else's, but no matter, guess what? You've got to forget the past, release forgiveness to the people who hurt you, and ask forgiveness for those you hurt; and then press on for the prize.

That day in Dallas I could have laid on the ground and felt sorry for myself. But victory doesn't come to the quitter. It comes to those who forget the past and press on (by faith) into the future. Let me give you a word that's coming from my heart to you, "Get Over It!" Get up, get off the ground. You may feel like a chump today, but you'll be "the champ" tomorrow. You may be in prison today, but you can be home soon, back in society, becoming all God has for you.

Don't let self pity or bitterness or depression rule over you any longer. Jesus loves you, and He has plans for your life to be blessed far beyond what you can possibly imagine. Champions are ordinary people that persevere when others have fallen and refuse to get up. Dallas was humiliating; Portland was exhilarating!

CHAMPIONS NEVER LOOK BACK!

James 1:12 *(net), "Happy is the one who endures testing, because when he has proven to be genuine, he will receive the crown of life that God promised to those who love Him."*

Why God Why?

————⚬⚬⚬————

Recently I was speaking at a Cowboy Church and I told the people a story about Herbert Theriot, the 1994 World Champion Calf Roper. Now don't hold me to the details, but the story goes something like this: It was the early nineties and Herbert was trying to qualify for the NFR at the end of the year. A flight that he was taking from Kansas City to San Francisco was cancelled - keeping him from competing at the cow Palace and probably going to the National Finals. It was extremely disappointing and Herbert started asking God, "Why?' "Why God? I prayed and it still didn't work out."

Not long after that Herbert's' good blue roan horse died. Again, he began to complain and ask, "Why?" The Spirit of God rose up inside of him and said, "Quit asking why, just begin to praise Me and allow Me to work in your life." **I Thessalonians 5:18** says, "In everything give thanks, for this is the will of God in Christ Jesus for you."

Well, Herbert began to do what the Lord spoke to him. He quit the 'Whys' and began to be thankful for the things God had blessed him with and began to thank Him in advance for the good things to come. Not long after 'Roany' died, roping legend Roy Cooper told Herbert, "I've got two horses you can ride." Those two horses fit Herbert like a glove. The rest is history. Herbert set a new single season record and became the World's Champion.

What's the bottom line? God wants to bless you. HE wants you to win! Jesus said, "In this world you shall have tribulations, but be of good cheer for I have overcome them." We need to rest in His ability and power to cause us to overcome. Quit judging your situation through natural vision. So you missed the NFR, when you go back you'll be at the top of the pack. So you lost your horse, two better ones are coming. So you lost your job, maybe it's time to start the business that you've always wanted to start. Maybe you lost your dog, a better dog is coming.

Remember the story in the book of Exodus? God had mightily delivered His people out of the hand of Pharaoh. No more slavery, just sweet freedom. However, when the Egyptian army closed in on them at the Red Sea, the people began to ask 'why.' "Why did You bring us out of Egypt, God - to destroy us? Why God, why?" Now, let me clarify something: God wants us to communicate with Him freely and openly. This includes questions of all kinds. However, the point here is that He doesn't want the spirit behind these questions to be fear, doubt, or anger.

Moses told them, "Stand still, hold your peace, and see the salvation of the Lord." Well you know the rest of the story. Their worst nightmare turned into possibly the most awesome miracle in the history of man. God wants you to let Him perform His best work in your life. **Romans 8:28** says, *"And we know that all things work together for good to those who love God, to those who are the called according to His purpose."*

We're not allowing Him to work all things together for good for us if we constantly question, complain, murmur and ask why. **Phil. 3:13**...*"forgetting those things which are behind and reaching forward to those things which are ahead..."*

Remember, God wants to bless you. Are you allowing Him to do that? Are you thanking Him in advance for taking you from your present difficult situation to the victory and joy that He has prepared for you? God is bigger than any difficulty you'll ever be confronted with. I encourage you to thank God, praise Him, and get happy! Watch Him come through for you.

GO FOR IT!

Herbert Theriot, Dean Oliver

Dream God's Dream

A few years ago I had an unusual experience. I was given a five gallon bucket full of baseballs. Baseballs? Yep. Don't ask me why. But it's true. I had no use personally for them so one by one I began to give them away; to kids mostly.

As the bucket slowly emptied I noticed that one of the balls was torn. I wouldn't give it away. As the months passed, the last of the balls were given away. Finally, there was one ball left, the torn one. I reached to the bottom of the barrel and pulled it out. To my suprise, for the first time, I noticed something was written on it. It was the only ball with writing on it.

As you can see it says "**Dream God's Dream**", what a message for you and I. What a message for man. I believe that God has a dream (plan) for every one of his creations. It is in our Father's heart, then He puts it in ours. The desire we have to pursue that dream is our confirmation that this dream comes from God's heart.

But hold it, you have some real flaws in your life don't you? Me too. We are earthen vessels, we are made of dirt. We are torn, like the ball, we're missing some stitches. Paul said, "the things I want to do I don't, the things I don't, I do. Oh wretched man that I am." But Paul didn't let his flaws keep him from fulfilling God's dream for his life. He realized that God works even stronger and greater when we are weak and even helpless.

Guess what? You may feel like you're the last ball in the bucket. No one wanted you, torn, flawed, and rejected. But hold it! You have something that none of the other balls had. You have something written on you. A message... *a message from heaven.* So, champion, are you willing to **Dream God's Dream** for your life? If you are, you will begin a "journey of faith with Jesus" like no other. Here's the key, don't ever stop believing! My favorite scripture is Isaiah 41:10 "*Fear not, for I am with you, be not dismayed, for I am your God. I will strengthen you, Yes, I will help you, I will uphold you with my victorious right hand.*"

Ouch! What was that? What's the needle and thread? The Great Healer, restorer, repairer, is putting new seams on you. Your ball is getting ready for your dream (the big leagues). The 100mph pitcher is rubbing you down and about to throw you into the strike zone of your destiny. Dreamers, play ball!

Peace at the Chute

As a boy growing up in the midst of rodeo, I can remember standing on the backside of many different bucking chutes around the country. My dad was a World Champion saddle bronc rider, and I always looked forward to seeing him ride. One thing that always amazed me about Dad was how cool and calm he was before he got on his horse.

Most of the other riders were getting a little hyper, or at least real serious about this time. Dad would be sitting on the back side of the chute with a buck rein in his hand, just visiting with somebody like he was at a Sunday picnic. Then, when he was up, he'd casually step over the chute and onto the horse.... Just another day at the office.

Yet, from a six year old's point of view, opening up that chute gate looked mighty wild and unpredictable. The horse might fall down in the chute, come out rearing straight up, go in any direction, or mash the rider up against the chute boards or pipes.

Life can be just like the bronc in the chute. You never know what the gate opening or a new day may bring. My dad was cool getting on a bucking horse, but other areas of his life were filled with strife and turmoil. Then in 1980, he gave his life to Jesus Christ. What a change, and what real peace came to him.

We live in a world that's very unpredictable. Jesus said, "You will hear of wars and rumors of wars. See that you are not troubled; for all these things must come to pass, but the end is not yet. For nation will rise against nation, and kingdom against kingdom. And there will be famines, pestilence, and earthquakes in various places." (Matt.24:6,7)

Sound familiar? What a peace to know that with Jesus Christ you're going to be able to ride through whatever challenges, difficulties, or potential disasters that come your way.

"So now, since we have been made right in God's sight by faith in His promise's, we can have real peace with Him because of what Jesus Christ our Lord has done for us." (Romans 5:1 Living Bible)

Do you have that peace that comes from knowing Him? You can, simply by believing God's word and asking Him to give you a new heart to live for Him.

Fearless

———∞∞∞———

For some time my neighbor Matt had wanted to ride saddle broncs. The opportunity came up for him to go to World Champion Tom Reeves bronc riding school in South Dakota for three days. Tom asked me to preach at the Sunday morning church service at the arena. I was excited to watch Matt and see all the future saddle bronc champs in the making. Every day I would lead a prayer over the school (and it better be a good one)!

Here's why - every year the Burch Rodeo Company would bring big stout horses to the school that had barely seen humans. Now, you've got to know from my perspective (a calf roper), I would rather get on a water buffalo or a grizzly bear than one of these horses. When the chute gate opened for these "rider-wanna-bees" it was rock n- ride - a combination of "holler Geronimo and help me Jesus!" How they survived 3 days with no major injuries was truly a sign of God's mercy and protection.

In light of these "very scary" conditions, I noticed a young bronc rider who seemed to be spectating all this. He was one of the students but he didn't seem to be making any move toward putting his new saddle on one of these horses. You could tell everything he owned was brand new - new vest, new bronc rein, new saddle. He had the new gear but something was missing - the courage to ride. Day one ended - no rides. Day 2 ended - still no attempts. Day 3 arrives - now it's all on the line! Well, guess what? He con-

Jeff with chimp
Madison Square Garden

tinued to watch others pursue their dreams; but he never budged! He was locked up in fear. He was so miserable and embarrassed! He had come all the way from California to South Dakota only to allow himself to be cheated out of his potential for greatness! Isn't fear a thief? John 10:10 (niv). "The thief comes only to steal and kill and destroy; I have come that they may have life, and have it to the full." Who knows, he might have been the best bronc rider at the school.

I read a book about a navy seal named Adam Brown. The book is called "Fearless." One of the things that caught my attention is that during training if someone decided to quit, there was a bell close by to ring. All you had to do was ring the bell and it was over! The pressure, the agony, the stress, the strain and the pain - over. In the case of our young bronc watcher - fear caused him to ring the bell before he even began!

I love this scripture; Romans 13:14 (Jubilee Bible 2000), "But be clothed with the Lord Jesus Christ and do not listen to the flesh, to fulfill its desires." As human beings the nature of our flesh is anything but courageous. It's God in us that truly gives us strength, wisdom, courage, optimism, and enthusiasm. We should "put on" Jesus like Sir Lancelot put on his best and most glorious battle armor. How do we actually do that? Number 1. Ephesians 6:10-18 encourages us to put on the whole armor of God. It's available! Number 2. - Studying and speaking God's word; meditating in faith brings His presence on you and your life. Proverbs 3:26 (God's Word Translation), "The Lord will be your confidence. He will keep your foot from getting caught." Knowing that HE is your strength, your protection - your ability - makes it time to Rock "N" Ride!

Don't forget champion - God wants you to win! Defeat paralyzing fear with the garment (the gifts) that He has given you. Don't spend your life watching others win! He wants you to win too! He loves you!

GO FOR IT!

Prov. 28:1 (nasb), *"The wicked flee when no one is pursuing, but the righteous are bold as a lion."*

Champions Slow Way Down

or several years I rodeoed competitively – traveling all over the U.S. and Canada. Like most hardcore rodeo guys, I was somewhat possessed to get to the next rodeo. It didn't seem to matter if I barely had enough time to get there or if I had lots of time. I was always pushing and pressing to get to the next rodeo.

Now, there are two sides to this coin. Obviously you need to stay focused and be diligent in what you are doing. But, the fact was, most of the time I could have stopped and looked at some historical landmarks, Grand Canyons, and a jillion other awesome tourist sites in North America. But, to be ruthlessly honest I was usually too selfish to be a blessing to my own family. Rodeo was all about me - my career, what I wanted to do, when I wanted to do It.! Most of it was conveniently disguised in "I've got to make a living." Yes, we do need to make a living, but we can give of ourselves to our mates, our children and others in the process.

I asked a golfer the other day "what's the very best golf tip you've ever gotten?" He didn't hesitate. He said, "Slow everything way down." I said, "OK, what's the best life tip you've ever had?" He smiled, "Slow everything way down!" In a world that sometimes feels like we're on a runaway train, that's probably some real sweet advice. We live in a society that seems to accelerate faster and faster. Cell phones, e-mails, and modern technology are a blessing in some ways, yet they seem to turn our daily schedules into whirlwinds.

Is life pushing you into a heart attack, a divorce, or some other disaster? Men – let's give our wives a real ear when we come home. Let's listen to our children and give them some quality time. Pull over to the next historical marker and read the whole thing. Yes, I know you might not be interested in the

1876 alligator attack on the settlers in Florida; but you can chase the dog around the car and have some fun!

Dad,– slowing down and spending quality time with your family is the most real and effective way you can show how much you love them! Are you ready?

Sloooow dooooown!

John 15:13 *(asv)*, *"Greater love hath no man than this, that a man lay down his life for his friends.*

Deb—Looking like he just won something!

Champions Forgive

⟨⟩⟨⟩⟨⟩

For years everything in my life revolved around rodeo and the desire to be a champion. So when Sherry and I were married in 1978 we had to work it around the Ellensburg rodeo. We were married by a creek in a beautiful pasture setting at our friend Jerry Anderson's ranch.

A regular part of the rodeo scenery in those days was rodeo preacher Glen Smith and his wife Ann. Glen had baptized us at the Cheyenne rodeo a month earlier. They were so awesome! In those days the first thing we'd do when we got to the rodeo was look for Glen and Ann's motor home. We were so excited about knowing Jesus and attending Bible studies in their motor home.

Glen and Ann were our moms and dads in the Spirit. One night just before the rodeo we were talking to them and we got on the subject of forgiveness. Now you've got to know that we were baby Christians and most everything about God was brand new to us. They encouraged us to get alone somewhere and ask the Holy Spirit to show us anyone that we needed to forgive or anything we needed to ask forgiveness for.

I was so excited about the Lord that I didn't want to wait; immediately I found the only private place I could find - the back of my horse trailer. As I knelt down in the hay, I had major doubts that I could hear the Holy Spirit speak to me. While kneeling, I had no more than started the sentence - "Lord is there anyone in my life that I need to forgive?" when I began to weep uncontrollably. A certain person jumped into my mind that had caused me much pain and hurt!

I began to see different scenarios in my life concerning this person and as I remembered more and more; I would release forgiveness over and over. This process lasted probably 30 to 40 minutes. I forgave and wept, forgave and wept, and wept some more. When I left my horse trailer, I was a different person. Jesus had set me free! The burden had lifted.

My friend Phil Doan had cowboy church in the Ranchman's Bar in Calgary, Alberta for many years. One Sunday at his church a Navaho lady from Arizona gave her testimony with an interpreter. She said her husband hated her, and finally in an attempt to kill her, he drove their car off a cliff near their home. It was a horrible wreck and both of them were killed. They woke up in hell and were not surprised because they had both rejected Jesus! However, they were shocked at the first person they saw in hell. It was the local pastor who was on fire for the Lord and had shared Jesus with them. They said to him, "we know why we're here; but why are you here?" The pastor tragically dropped his head and said, "there was someone that I wouldn't forgive." He went to an eternal hell because there was someone he would not forgive! Hard to believe? It's scriptural - Jesus said, "If you don't forgive others, I can't forgive you." The Native American lady came back to life and became a Christian.

P.S. You can be sure there is no one on the planet that she won't forgive!

Has someone hurt you? Maybe they stole something precious from you, or were part of a plot to destroy you. Satan loves to set up traps of ugly life situations that he hopes will snare you in bitterness, hatred and unforgiveness. He knows the only way you can escape is to (get in your horse trailer) your secret place, kneel down and ask the Holy Spirit to reveal what's in your heart.

Christian, forgiveness is your key to freedom! Here's a key to forgiveness. No one (including Jesus) said you would forget what happened to you; but you don't have to forget it to forgive! You don't have to feel all lovey-dovey about that person or situation. What you must do though is forgive by faith and let the Lord do a healing in your heart that only He can do.

Think about it! Jesus gave us this commandment. He said in John 13:34 (nkjv), "A new commandment I give unto you, that you love one another; as I have loved you, that you also love one another." When we hold unforgiveness toward someone or something, we are doing the exact opposite of love. We are letting anger and murder rule in our hearts. **I John 4:8** says, *"God* *is love."* When we turn away from love, we turn from God, His nature and His way of operating. We begin to suffer when this happens as well as the people around us. God's will and plan for our lives is to be vessels of His love.

P.S. Here's something pretty crazy! When you hold unforgiveness - you're the only one that will suffer. The person you're angry with may not even know that you're mad. Then they go on down life's highway whistling Dixie and you put yourself in a self imposed prison.

Here's a tip that could really help you consistently walk in forgiveness. "This isn't about your feelings. You don't have to feel anything! Forgive in faith and ask the Lord to help you." You can be honest with the Lord and tell Him - "Lord I'm so angry at this person or situation; but I choose to forgive - not because I feel like it but because I love You and want to obey your word. I don't want to live in chains!

Set Yourself Free Champion!

I John 1:9 *(asv), "If we confess our sins, He is faithful and righteous to forgive us our sins, and to cleanse us from all unrighteousness."*

Matt 6:14 *(amp), "For if you forgive people their trespasses (their reckless and willful sins, leaving them. letting them go, and giving up resentment), your heavenly Father will also forgive you."*

Cowboy Church on hay bales Granbury, Texas 1990

The American

〜〜〜

herry and I are sitting in the Dallas Cowboys football stadium. This is one big place! Today it isn't about football though, it's rodeo, and rodeo at its finest. Cowboys and cowgirls that are competing represent 140 world champion gold belt buckles. One by one they introduce the competitors and honor their accomplishments. You could cut the air with a knife!

A young Texas calf roper backs his horse into the box while the crowd noise and background music is deafening. Are you ready for this? He's about to rope, flank and tie his calf in 7.5 seconds and win a whopping $600,000! What? That's right - $600,000. Earlier we saw a young bareback rider win $600,000 also. As we sat and watched this event unfold, I realized I had hoped for this and worked toward something like this my whole life!

Rodeo has blossomed - its finally come into its own. The event is called "THE AMERICAN" and this is the second year. Last year a young bareback rider named Richard Champion won one million, one hundred thousand dollars! The rodeo is sponsored by RFD TV and is truly an excellent event.

Now, let's roll the clock back some forty plus years. My dad and I, Casey Tibbs, Harley May, and several other cowboys gathered together with some high powered business people. We were meeting at the Century Plaza Hotel on Rodeo Drive in Los Angeles. The purpose was to devise a way to promote rodeo's top cowboys and cowgirls in an environment of super rodeos. Each event would be televised, adding prize money that would elevate rodeo to a higher financial plain. Try as hard as we could, somehow it never quite happened. Through the years multiple attempts by different people were made to do something similar, but to no avail.

In the book of **Ecclesiastes 3:1**, it says, *"There is a time for everything and a time for every purpose under heaven."* As I sat and watched this great competition unfold; my mind wandered back to being a young boy surrounded by great champion cowboys in my dad's era. I was spurred on by them to become a champion myself. Little did my dad and I know that our careers and the careers of others were pioneering the future of rodeo. Our dreams to make a good living rodeoing were the plow that broke up the fallowed ground to sow the seeds of the future.

Life has seasons and all of us are pioneering whether we know it or not. Maybe you're the first one in your family to receive Jesus as your Lord and Saviour. Your own family and close friends may be making fun of you. They call you a Bible thumper or a "holy roller." Words can hurt for sure, but you must realize that as you keep on hacking through the jungle with your machete, you are building a safe road, a path for others to walk on that leads to heaven.

When you love the Lord and live for Him unashamedly - people may misunderstand you, slander, or attack you; but the truth is - your life is the foundation for future generations to stand on. Let's pretend something - you ready? You're sitting in a large place - a very large place - bigger than Cowboys stadium. You are at a huge event. The Bible calls it "the supper of the lamb." God's champions are there with you - they are being introduced - stories are told of the great feats and the championship performances of His Saints. You've waited your whole life for this day! Now the reward is here. There is a reward (a big reward) for serving God - for being faithful - to hold your course for a lifetime. Swimming upstream against the current of sin in this world and overcoming spiritual giants while doing everything you possibly can to bring people into the kingdom has finally led you to this moment! Joy unspeakable! If that isn't incredible enough, your Heavenly Father looks at you with a huge smile and says **"Well done good and faithful servant!"**

Colossians 3:23-24, *God's Word translation, "Whatever you do, do it wholeheartedly as though you were working for your real master and not merely for humans. You know that your real master will give you an inheritance as your reward. It is Christ, your real master, whom you are serving."*

Sylvester

⸻ ◆◆◆ ⸻

*I*t was the end of June 1985 and I was in Reno, Nevada. Reno always seemed like the launching pad for the summer rodeo run. My National Finals Rodeo calf roper friend, Sylvester Mayfield walked up to me and asked me if he could ride my horse at the Calgary Stampede. Sylvester (we call him "Silver") was one of the most explosive ropers of his era. As I told him "sure Silver"- the Lord dropped a word in my heart, "pray with him every time before he ropes."

So, two weeks later we're in Calgary, home of the $50,000 roping. I walked up to Sylvester before he roped and prayed with him. I prayed that the Lord would protect him and Sting (my horse), and that the Lord would be with him in a special way. We were obedient to pray through his first three runs. He placed in the average and qualified for the top 10 on Sunday. Calgary's format then was the first 10 ropers roped one calf then the fastest four roped a second calf. Things were really exciting that day; not just for Sylvester, but for me too. The horse owner gets 25% of the prize. Well, here's where the story gets a little wild.

Sylvester roped his first calf and he ended up in fifth place. No good – one hole out. Sylvester took my horse, Sting, back to the barn- a long way from the rodeo arena. He unsaddled him and was heading for a taxi to leave the rodeo grounds. But wait. One of the top four ropers broke the barrier but the line judge failed to communicate the plus 10 seconds for breaking the barrier to the timers in the announcers stand. Back at the

Sylvester winning $50,000 at the 1985 Calgary Stampede

roping chute we were wondering why they hadn't corrected the barrier mistake. I thank the Lord that I married a real faith woman. God put it in Sherry's heart, "don't give up – keep believing!"

The judge finally realized that sure enough the cowboy in fourth place had broken the barrier and that meant Sylvester was in the final four ropers to go for the $50,000. Sherry heard the judge's decision first and said, "I'll try to find Sylvester; and you'll have to saddle Sting." Sherry caught a ride in a 4-wheeler around the grounds over to the rodeo office, a long way. By now Sylvester has his traveling clothes on – sneakers, cutoffs and T-shirt; and he's getting into a taxi – about 10 seconds from being gone. She hollers "Sylvester, get your cowboy gear on, you made it to the final four!"

Now, you've gotta know that basically nothing gets Sylvester excited, but this was definitely an exception. He grabbed his cowboy clothes, got on the 4-wheeler with Sherry and they go racing back to the rodeo arena. At the same time all this is going on I'm saddling Sting in world record time; and galloping for the arena. We got there about 2 minutes before it's time for Silver to rope. He was the first roper. Two other guys were helping us, and we were all putting ropes, jerk line, skid boots on the horse, etc. It looked like a Nascar pit crew. Yet in the midst of all this craziness, God gave me the grace to do what He said to do in Reno. Pray before every calf! We did! – not a long prayer though!

You can see in the picture, he ropes sharp and is half way down the rope before the calf turns around. He ties his calf in 9.1 – which is great; but we've got 3 other ropers. One by one they have different kinds of trouble. Can you believe it? Silver wins the $50,000!! I'm surprised that Hollywood didn't jump on this tale.

This story speaks to my heart because so many times in life it looks like we've been eliminated in our quest to win. There are so many things in life that can cause you to "go for the taxi". We could have quit that day and given up on God. We could have said, "well, this is the hand I've been dealt; there's nothing more that I can do." How about this? Keep believing God – stay in the game. Consider these scriptures: *"For with God nothing will be impossible."* (**Luke 1:37**) *But thanks be to God, who gives us the victory through our Lord Jesus Christ.* (**1 Corinthians 15:57**) God loves you incredibly, and HE wants you to win!

NEVER GIVE UP CHAMPION!

Three School Give-Away

***

Jt was March of 1982 and I was driving from Texas to Alberta, Canada. I was going to put on three free calf roping schools; and then compete at the Edmonton Super Rodeo. This was especially cool for me because I hadn't entered any rodeos for 3 years.

Sherry and I were so excited about receiving the Lord in our hearts (in 1978) that we had shut down everything else in the world so that we could spend literally hundreds of hours learning God's Word. We were caught up in (His)"training camp." We would go to churches, conferences, revivals; or anywhere we could find to know God better. This period lasted for over three years. Looking back, it truly prepared us for the years and plans that lay ahead of us.

Our special friend Glenn Thompson had advertised and organized all these schools. He worked so hard! What a champion! The first school was at Jake Brauns arena in Beechy, Saskatchewan - where? Not a metropolis. Forty six ropers came to that school. We worked hard - really hard! I wanted this school to be a blessing to these guys. Evening came and I gathered everyone around in a circle and I told them what happened to me, when I won the world's championship. I went back to the motel room and sat on the edge of my bed. I looked at my new gold belt buckle and said, "Is that all there is?"

I told them it was great to see a lifelong goal fulfilled; but it didn't fill the void in my heart. Little did I know then that only Jesus could fill that place. Many of these ropers gave their lives to the Lord that day! Was I ever pumped! It was like my life had a purpose and a value that I had never known before.

The second school was at Lethbridge, Alberta; and there were 110 students. That's right! I had several guys helping me and we would put 10 ropers in a station with an instructor.

A three ring (roper) circus, and it was incredible. An intense time to enter the hearts of these guys dreams and pour out our knowledge, passion and love into helping them.

At the end of the day I gathered everyone at one end of the arena and shared Jesus with them. Tuffy Tail Feathers, a Native American cowboy walked up to me afterwards and asked if we had any cowboy Bibles. I told him, "sure Tuffy." Two weeks later Tuffy was killed in a car wreck! I'm sure he gave his life to the Lord that day. That made the whole trip more than worthwhile. Many others made decisions to receive Jesus!

Then on to the third school - just outside of Edmonton. There were only 8 or 9 ropers there, but it was probably the most significant school of all. There were Native American ropers from several different reservations. Meeting and connecting with them opened the door to having roping schools all over western Canada for the next four years.

Schools were over now and on to the Super Rodeo. Without telling you the whole story, I will tell you that after not competing for three years, God gave me the grace to rope well and win the calf roping at Edmonton. It really put a stamp on our free-school trip to Canada!. Looking back I can see that Jesus had a definite purpose and plan for all these schools, and the Edmonton Rodeo. It was a privilege for me to share the good news with cowboys in Canada!

Here's a side story. Financially when I got to Beechy - all the way from Ft. Worth, Texas, I asked my friend Glenn if he had gas money to get us to Lethbridge. He said sure, why? I told him I had exactly $.46 cents in my pocket. He couldn't believe it and said, "You've come all the way from Texas and you've got 46 cents?" I told him, "That's cutting it a little close isn't it?" Get this: before I left Canada, God had blessed me with a win at Edmonton and a paid roping school in Southern Alberta. I headed back to Texas with $5,000 in my front pocket. A lot of money in 1982. Jesus said if we put His kingdom first, He would add everything we need in this world. My paraphrase is: He will bless you like no one can when you put Him first. (**Matthew 6:33**)

OK champion, what gifts, talents, resources, ideas, plans etc. do you have that could bless people and help them to come to know Jesus or know Him better? There's nothing like the excitement and joy of launching out in faith to touch others with the love of Jesus! Real love unlocks the doors of people's hearts.

GO FOR IT!

Matt 6:33 *(nkjv), "But seek first the kingdom of God and His righteousness, and all these things shall be added to you."*

Super School at Morley, Alberta, Canada

The Cow

~~~

It was 1989 and we were having Cowboy Church at the old auction barn in the Ft. Worth Stockyards. It was Wednesday in January; and it was major cold. If you've never been to Texas in the winter, you may not know just how cold it can get. The humidity was about 80% and the temperature was approximately 30 degrees. Only those that were excited to learn about the Lord showed up that particular night since the auction arena was not heated.

We were having a little praise and worship music when someone came out of the back of the auction ring and said, "There's a cow down back here, it looks like someone has left her to die." We took timeout of church and went back to check her out. Because it was so cold in the open air, the first thing we did was drag her into the auction ring area where it was a little warmer.

Now, you have to picture the people (about 20) that were there that night. Most of them were fairly new Christians who were very excited about their new walk with God. They had been learning what the word of God had to say about anything and everything in life. So, when the first person said, "Let's pray healing for this cow;" everyone immediately gathered around her and prayed. Then our church drummer came up with a great idea. Let's load the cow in his work van so she can get warm, and he can haul her home. No small endeavor. As crazy as this may sound, we decided to go for it! After great difficulty we got the van in the little auction ring; and then after much greater difficulty about eight of us guys managed to lift and slide her into the van.

Here's the hilarious part-- we sat her up on her haunches with her head up. She was looking through the window. Needless to say church was all "about the cow" that night. Sherry and I drove around the van as we were leaving the stockyards and saw the cow turn her head toward us. I wondered if she was wanting to say to all of us, "Thanks for praying and caring for me! Thanks for not giving up when everyone else had. I'm warm and I've got a chance to make it now."

One way or another the call of God for all of us is to give our lives for the lives of others. That's what our savior did for us. Freely you received, freely give.   God Bless. (Isaiah 58:6).

GOD BLESS!

Isaiah 58:6, *"Is not this the fast that I have chosen? to loose the bands of wickedness, to undo the heavy burdens, and to let the oppressed go free, and that ye break every yoke?"*

Out Of The Chute

by Earnest Tooke

In the mid 1940's, Joe Kelsey, a Washington rodeo producer, shipped in a load of range horses from Cragston, Alberta, Canada. That load brought a horse that developed into one of the Northwest's greatest bucking horses. Part Shire, brown in color, and weighing 1300 pounds; his name was Snake. His was a wild style of bucking; he would throw his head back in the rider's face, drop his shoulders, and kick off to the side, ducking and twisting and turning back. A rider could watch Snake buck 15 or 20 times and wouldn't have had any idea for a game plan. Snake didn't follow a set pattern; he just bucked as hard as he could and unloaded every bronc rider who tried him.

Joe Kelsey furnished rodeo stock at the 1949 Penticton, British Columbia, rodeo. One of the cowboys entered was an up- and-coming young bronc rider, Deb Copenhaver. Deb hadn't been in rodeo very long, but he was winning his share of prize money in the saddle bronc event. Born in 1925 and a native of the Northwest, he grew up in the Creston, Washington area and entered his first rodeo when he was 15. He joined the U.S. Navy Seabees when he was 17 and spent two years in North Africa during World War II. After Deb was discharged from the service, he returned to Washington and went to work driving a bulldozer in a logging camp. Working full time and rodeoing whenever he could, Deb won second place in the 1946 Northwest Amateur Bucking contest at Pendleton. In 1947, Deb entered nine rodeos and won the all-around at Wilbur, Washington. Rodeoing as a career was looking better all the time, so in '48' Deb quit his logging job, loaded his chaps and bronc saddle, and headed up the road.

When Deb checked the draw posted for the bronc riding at Pendleton, Or. he found himself matched with the mighty Snake. Deb's bronc ride was sensational; he handled every terrible jump, twist, and turn that the horse could throw at him. After 10 violent and action-filled seconds, the whistle blew, and Deb Copenhaver went into the record book as the first bronc rider to successfully ride Snake. The ride catapulted Deb to instant fame. Overnight his name was known to everyone familiar with rodeo throughout the United States and Canada.

Deb Copenhaver and Casey Tibbs were the two top saddle bronc riders of the 1950's. In 1951, Deb finished second to Casey for the world championship. Casey was first in '52, and Deb was second. In 1954, and it must have seemed frustrating to Deb, Casey again was champion, and Deb was second. Finally, in 1955, Deb Copenhaver was world champion saddle bronc rider, beating out "Ol' Case" by $174.

Deb on Snake in Penpicton, B.C.

In 1956, Deb won his second world title with a comfortable $7,000 lead over George Menkenmeier. Deb finished in fourth place in championship standings for 1958; that was his last year of full-time rodeo competition. In addition to two world championships, Deb won the bronc riding at Madison Square Garden, Cheyenne, and Pendleton.

If a list of the best saddle bronc riders of all time were drawn up, Deb Copenhaver's name would be on the list. Likewise, Snake would be named as one of the best saddle broncs; if there had been a Bucking Horse of the Year award in Snake's time, he would have been a cinch to win it.

Finishing Strong

〜〜〜〜

By Deb Copenhaver

*H*aving spent the last half of my life walking with the Lord and comparing it with the first half, (when I was not) gives me a fairly good perspective on the blessings available when we commit our lives to Him. My main focus now is going from this life to the next – and how I finish.

Before I was living for the Lord, I competed whole heartedly with fierce and great determination to be the very best bronc rider I could be. I was giving everything that was in me, disciplining my mind and body to be a world

champion. My goal to win that 'top prize', to obtain the crown, which was a perishable one at best.

Now as a Christian, I need to contend for that imperishable crown/prize with the same zeal, discipline and determination. I must persevere with certainty; not allowing the enemy to distract my focus with whatever negative situations this life throws at me. I'm not looking back but keeping my eyes fixed on the goal that lies ahead – the prize of heaven – and finishing strong!

Deb Copenhaver

The Chapel

⸺⚬⚬⚬⸺

I f you head west of Spokane, Washington on Highway 2; in about one hour you'll be in my dad's hometown of Creston, Washington. On the east side of town you'll drive by the coolest little log chapel. If you pull in and go inside, you'll not only be amazed at this little pristine structure; but you will sense a real presence of the Lord there!

It was the mid "90s," and my dad flew from Washington to my house in Granbury, Texas. We had a dream to build a log church and Dad had come to help us. We had moved Cowboy Church from the Ft. Worth Stockyards and now we wanted to build a log church in Granbury, Texas. For sure, dreams are infectious! While Dad was there being a part of our dream, God was putting something special in his heart - a vision to build a roadside chapel (a God stop) on Highway 2 in Washington. Here's the thing - when God puts a dream in your heart - if you will trust Him and launch out, He will help you bring it to pass!

Building the chapel was a labor of love and a product of faith. From the logs that were milled out of telephone poles, to wooden shingles made from those logs, to the doors, windows, and even a "bronze praying cowboy" in the parking lot (made by my sister Debbie, who is a renowned bronze artist). Dad and Cheryl had been standing looking at the roof wondering what to put on it when Vester Sitton walked up and said "shake it." That meant let's put wood shakes on it and use the logs dad already had to make them. Their prayer was answered and paid for. Every phase was provided by God through His people.

My stepmom Cheryl has poured her love into the chapel. She has planted flowers and plants and spent countless hours making the grounds a little piece of heaven. Inside the chapel is a sign-in book where people not only put their names and addresses; but make a comment on what the chapel meant to them. Many state what's going on in their lives and prayers that they prayed "in the chapel." The chapel is never locked; so sometimes a hitch hiker will spend the night there. No problem!

Recently my dad went out to the chapel and found someone sound asleep inside. Dad said the guy looked exhausted. His name was Wyatt and he had a skate board next to him. Guess what, Wyatt started on the east coast and was skate boarding all across America. His reason for such a journey was: "America, please come back to God!" Dad drove back to his house and got bedding and pillows for him. Cheryl made him supper and Dad brought it all back to the chapel. They prayed God would give Wyatt the strength and grace to finish his journey! The next day they happened to look out their window just as Wyatt was heading down the highway on his skate board. Mission accomplished!

Did you know the Bible says that when you become a Christian (asking Jesus into your heart) that you become God's temple where He lives? Can I change this just a little? You really become His "chapel." **I Cor. 3:16**, *"Don't you realize that all of you together are the temple of God and that the Spirit of God lives in you?"* People are entering your life (your chapel) everyday. They come in with every life scenario. You are there to listen, help, encourage and bring a sweet presence of God to the weary traveler! Hope and strength when none remains!

Yes, miracles happen in the chapel. Just like the little log chapel God made in Washington; God made you with great love and care. **Psalm 139** says, *"you were perfectly and wonderfully made."* Your life was meant to touch multitudes of people. The front door of your life is never locked. God's love flows freely in and out.

HIS LOVE IS REAL IN YOU!

GO FOR IT!!

P.S. Here's a personal invitation - if you're ever on Hwy 2 heading west of Spokane, Washington - Stop -Rest- and pray.

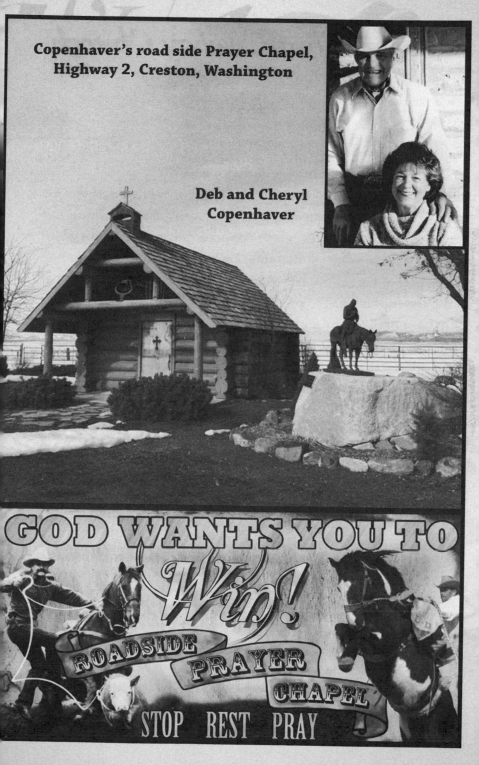

Copenhaver's road side Prayer Chapel, Highway 2, Creston, Washington

Deb and Cheryl Copenhaver

GOD WANTS YOU TO *Win!*

ROADSIDE PRAYER CHAPEL

STOP REST PRAY

Worlds First Cowboy Church
30th anniversary celebration 1986-2016

C hurch in a bar, can you believe it? Not only a bar but the biggest honky-tonk in the world!

How did that happen? Well, it was the fall of 1985 and everything was changing. I had been teaching calf roping schools all over North America; but suddenly they had come to a halt. During that time I was president of the Cowboy Chapter of the Fellowship of Christian Athletes; and part of that job description was to preach at the first National Finals Rodeo in Las Vegas. Sherry and I were praying and seeking God for His plan for our lives. Little did we know what He had in store.

In Vegas on Saturday before church I met Billy Bob Barnett (who owned Billy Bob's) and his manager Tex Whitson (who was formerly Merle Haggard's manager). I invited them to the coliseum church service the next morning. That Saturday

Jeff and Sherry at Billy Bobs Texas

was Billy Bob's birthday; so I didn't expect them to show. However, Tex said, "I'll be there." Surprisingly he showed up, but he looked like it was a real short night. That morning we were informed that we had 38 minutes for the entire service. Susie Mc Entire (Reba's sister) sang awesome (as always). My calf roper friend Broadus Gravette gave his testimony and I preached. Well, God was there and Tex came up to me after the service and asked me to come and see him when I got home in Ft. Worth. Long story short; when I met with Tex in Ft. Worth, he asked me if I would have church at Billy Bob's in their bull riding arena. The bar has a bull riding arena in it! It would be for 3 weeks during the Ft. Worth Rodeo in January, 1986. We called it Cowboy Church and we had three awesome services. Champion cowboys Bruce Ford, Bobby Del Vecchio and others gave their testimonies.

Jeff and Tex Whitson

Over 200 people attended those services weekly. Some were "sure-nuff" cowboys and cowgirls and some were just curious of what was going on. What they heard was the Good News of Jesus Christ, that God loved them and He wanted to have a personal relationship with them. In the three Stock Show Sundays at Billy Bob's, dozens made professions of faith. It was a glorious beginning, and it prompted Tex Whitson to ask me if I wanted to keep having services every Sunday. He came up to me and said, "Jeff, I think we're supposed to keep having church." I told him, "I agree," and the rest is history. " Cowboy Church" was born!

Now, for history's sake let me clarify something. Up to this time there were Cowboy Church meetings all over the country - at rodeos, fairs, horse shows, etc, etc. Men like Glenn Smith, Coy Huffman, Ted Pressley, Dennis McKinley, Wilbur Plaugher, Mark Schricker, Walt Arnold, myself and others were pioneering a great move of God. However, Cowboy Church at Billy Bob's was the first ongoing weekly church that began what we know today as Cowboy Church. God was doing a new thing! We had church in Billy Bob's for two years, then the old auction barn and then the Stockyards hotel. Historically, Ft. Worth is known as "the place where the west begins." In light of that, it's pretty special that the "World's First Cowboy Church" started in the old Ft. Worth Stockyards.

One Sunday I was preaching (in the bull riding arena) on the subject of being willing to give away what God has given you. I surprised myself when I kicked my right boot off - all the way to the back row of chairs. A man stood up and caught my boot in the air and immediately put it on. He hollered, it fits perfectly! By then I kicked my other boot back to him. On it went! The boots he wore to church that day had big holes in the soles. The happy look on his face spoke to us all. God is real - He loves me - He will do anything for me!

In the early years when we were in Billy Bob's, little did we know that people would come to one of our services and then go home and start a Cowboy Church in a bar, auction barn, hotel, a feed store, or any number of other creative places to have church. Also, while we were at Billy Bob's, we had all kinds of rodeo arena events at Cowtown Coliseum which is immediately next door to Billy Bob's - stick horse rodeos for kids, rodeo schools, bull ridings, rodeos, ropings, etc. It was awesome! Following this pattern, most Cowboy Churches today have arenas next to the church to hold their outreach events.

One year after we started, Canadian Hall of Fame Cowboy, Phil Doan, began weekly services in the Ranchman's Bar in Calgary, Alberta. They were the second Cowboy Church. Joanne Cash Yates (Johnny Cash's sister) and her husband Harry Yates came to speak at Calgary and they were so excited

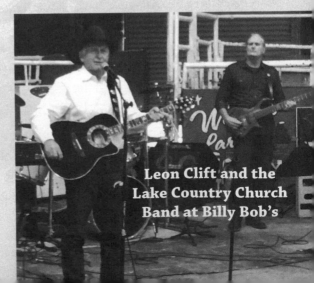

Leon Clift and the Lake Country Church Band at Billy Bob's

about Cowboy Church that they went home to Nashville, Tennessee to have Cowboy Church in the Sweetwater lounge at the Holiday Inn. That was the third Cowboy Church and boy did it spread from there! There are hundreds, probably thousands of Cowboy Churches world wide today.

Through the years people have asked us "What was the first Cowboy Church like?" The first cowboy church was a training camp for champions. We called the preaching "no bull gospel." God loves you - you are His champion. He has great things for your life. Contrary to what many may think, Cowboy Church was never an ethnic church designed to reach cowboys. There was never a big percentage of cowboys at our services; nor is there today. Our dress code was "come as you are." We wanted people to feel comfortable in clothes they were used to wearing.

Buckaroo church leader Jim Ryder and Jeff.

We were more concerned with their souls than their style. Cowboy Church pointed people toward a love relationship with Jesus Christ and the Holy Spirit. We saw God save, heal and deliver His people to live great lives for Him. I had trained champion ropers for years. Now, God put me in a position to train and encourage His people to fulfill the destiny and plans that He had placed in them before the foundation of the world! Everyone was so excited - experiencing their new life in Christ.

TO GOD BE THE GLORY!

This scripture seems to describe "Cowboy Church" in those early days:

Acts 4:13, *"Now as they observed the confidence of Peter and John and understood that they were uneducated and untrained men; they were amazed, and began to recognize them as having been with Jesus..."*

The good news we were sharing was coming out of our hearts and touching others. In October of 2016, we celebrated the 30th anniversary of World's First Cowboy Church, at the original site - Billy Bob's Texas - Ft. Worth's Historic Stockyards.

Praying time at Billy Bob's

Church service held at honky-tonk

By LAURA YEE
Star-Telegram Writer

So, what's shaking at Billy Bob's Texas, Fort Worth's leading honky-tonk, on Sunday morning? Church.

What? Sounded like you said church.

Yep. Church.

Sure enough. Cowboys from Cowtown and the curious who went to Billy Bob's for cow church Sunday didn't think it was anything out of the ordinary. Even if the preaching came from the club's rodeo arena and the women wearing high-heeled shoes had trouble walking on the dirt.

"It doesn't matter where it sat," said Carroll Pelton, wearing his cowboy hat and boots as he sat on the gates normally reserved for exiting steers. "It's even better than having it in a church. You'd see people just drive on by, but 'cause it's here, you got people who don't always go to church on Sunday comin' in."

Pelton, who was with his daughter and wife, were among more than 250 other people filling the bleachers and the chairs in the middle of the nightclub's rodeo arena to attend the first Christian service at Billy Bob's.

Dennis McKinley, president of

Star-Telegram/MARK GAIL

Jeff Copenhaver

Western World Mission and co-sponsor, said the service was at Billy Bob's Texas to highlight the Southwestern Exposition and Fat Stock Show and to prove that people can pray and find God anywhere, even in a rodeo arena.

He said use of the arena was free, and another service will be offered at 11 a.m. next Sunday.

Star-Telegram/MARK G...

Crowd at Billy Bob's listens to church service.

Jeff Copenhaver, minister and president of the Cowboy Chapter of Christian Athletes and the other sponsor, gave the service in a black Western hat, jeans and boots while people were playing pool and video games a few yards away.

"Welcome to cow church," he said.

"It's nice just to be here acknowledging God with or without the stained-glass windows," Copenhaver told the churchgoers while standing beneath huge advertising signs that frame the arena.

Sitting in the bleachers watching others pray was Patricia Palmer, who was visiting Fort Worth.

She said the idea of having a Christian service in a rodeo arena w... humbling.

After testimony from st... wrestlers Bobby DelVechio a... Paul Luchsinger, and songs... Luchsinger's wife, Susie Mc... tire, a collection was taken ... cowboy hats.

"Our special friend Champion roper Dennis McKinley, helped us with Cowboy Church, Youth Rodeo Association - "The Masters Championships", and has been a Gospel pioneer to the cowboy world. Thanks Dennis - You're a Champ!"

I'll Be Your Huckleberry!

I love the movie Tombstone. The other night it came on again and I hollered to Sherry that the best scene in the whole movie was right then. Johnny Ringo, a hot dog bad guy was meeting Wyatt Earp for a showdown. Ringo was known to be the fastest gun in the territory. To challenge or face him was pure suicide. He was death with boots, hat and a gun.

Wyatt had just visited Doc Holiday and Doc's tuberculosis was so bad that Doc couldn't get out of bed. Well, Ringo gets to the appointed showdown place and out of the shadow of a big tree walks Doc Holiday. What's going on? As Doc walks forward, he says, "I'll be your huckleberry"; which means, "Here I am, I'm not afraid of you; let's do it!" Ringo starts to choke because he knows he can outdraw Wyatt, but Doc could be another story. He can see Doc is not intimidated. They begin to back up in a circle waiting for someone to make a move. Then, Ringo goes for his gun and Doc outdraws him - shoots and kills him. About this time Wyatt gets there and realizes that his friend Doc has stepped in and saved his life. You can see that Wyatt is wondering how Doc got out of bed. Doc grins and says "I wasn't quite as sick as I let on."

How humbling and yet how incredible for a man to lay down his life for his friend.

I John 15:13 says, *"Greater love has no one than this, than to lay down one's life for his friends." Proverbs 18:24 tells us, "But there is a friend (Jesus) who sticks closer than a brother."*

Satan had trapped the entire human race when Adam and Eve fell to sin. Now, he is the Johnny Ringo of the earth. But hold it, who's that being crucified on that tree on your behalf? Jesus Christ, Son of the Living God! He says to satan, "I'll be your huckleberry." Satan, your era of terror is over. I've come to destroy death, hell and the grave. You've bullied mankind long enough with fear, dread and torment. It is finished! I'm stepping in for my friends." He then spoiled satanic powers and principalities as He paid the ultimate sacrifice for your life with His own. How humbling and yet how incredible for Jesus to lay down His life for us; His Friends.

I just got done watching the movie "Passion of the Christ." It had been several years since I'd seen it and I guess I had forgotten just how real they portrayed what Jesus went through before and during the cross. The whipping He underwent was more than a whipping. The historian Josephus wrote that you could see Jesus' lungs from the back after the Romans tore strip after strip of flesh from His back. His face and body were beaten beyond recognition. Have you ever been cut on the forehead? You bleed like your throat has been cut. Can you imagine the river of blood that flowed from that crown of giant thorns? What a price Jesus paid to bear your sins and mine.

Scripture says He could have called 10,000 angels at any moment and freed Himself from all this pain, agony and torment. Instead He pressed on through an unbelievable nightmare to win our salvation. He chose to do this for us. Acknowledging and accepting the sacrificial gift of God's son is the most important decision and act that you will make this side of eternity. He did it just for you. Glory to His Wonderful Name! Forever we can praise the champion of the universe and shout – Jesus! Jesus, Jesus!

Back to Tombstone, Wyatt is at Doc's death bed. They had more or less said their goodbyes; and Doc asked him to leave.

As Wyatt stood up and started to walk away, he turned around and said, "Thanks for always being there for me, Doc." Maybe right now would be a good time to tell the Lord, "Thank you for always being there for me – past, present and for eternity. Show me Lord how to walk with you and serve you – how to be a Huckleberry for others."

GOD BLESS

Jesus carrying your sin...

Receive Him and Win.

Champions Know They Must Be Entered

﹏﹏﹏∞∞∞﹏﹏﹏

For several years now, rodeo announcers have been using the "cowboy prayer" to start many of the rodeos around the country. The prayer goes something like this: "One of these days when we ride into that beautiful land (Heaven) where the water's sweet, the grass is green and stirrup high, He (God) will tell us that our entry fees are paid."

Anyone who has rodeoed knows that if the entries close at 12:00 noon, and you call in to enter at 12:01, it's just too bad, partner. It makes no difference why you called late. . .your house burned down. . .someone kidnapped you . . .you had to stop and save a girl scout troop from being run over by a truck. . .all good reasons to call in late. The entry operator will probably congratulate you on your heroics, and then reply, "I'm sorry, the entries have closed, there's nothing I can do for you."

It's great to have someone pay your fees, but that doesn't do you one speck of good if you didn't call in and enter the rodeo. The Bible says that through Adam's sin all mankind is born into sin; which means separation from God . . . **Romans 3:23** - *"All have sinned and come short of the glory of God*, "John3:16 . . . *God so loved the world that He gave His only begotten Son, that whosoever should believe in Him should not perish but have everlasting life."* **(John 3:16)**. For God so loved us that He paid our fees by sending Jesus to die for us.

Now the question is, "Have you called on God, received the sacrifice of His Son, and made Him your savior and Lord? Is your name in the Lamb's Book of Life - God's entry sheet?" On judgment day there will be folks with lots of excuses. . .I was a good ol' boy. . I was a good family man. . .I never hurt anyone. . .I helped people and did good works. . .My friends would have made fun of me. . .I was always so busy, etc., etc., etc.

When the Son of man (Jesus) comes in His glory. . .all the nations will be gathered before Him, and He will separate them one from another, as a Shepherd divides His sheep from the goats. And He will set the sheep on His right hand, but the goats on the left. Then the King will say to those on His right hand, "Come, you blessed of My Father, inherit the kingdom prepared for you from the foundation of the world." Then He will also say to those on the left hand, "Depart from me, You cursed, into the everlasting fire prepared for the devil and his angels." (**Matthew 25: 31-41**). To those who have their name in the "Entry Book," there will be great joy as they enter into eternity. Their entry fees have been paid, and they entered before the books closed (death).

This is the big one, the daddy of 'em all - bigger than Houston, Calgary, or Cheyenne. This is eternity, it's forever. For sure, your entry fees have been paid. . .but have you entered?!

GO FOR IT!

Cowboys circled up in prayer, Warwick, Queensland, Australia

Prayer of Salvation

------ ⌘ ------

Where will you hang your hat for eternity?

God wants you to receive His free gift of salvation. If you have never invited Jesus, the Prince of Peace, to be your Lord and Savior, I invite you to pray this prayer.

Father,

You loved the world so much, You gave Your only Son to die for our sins so that whoever believes in Him will not perish, but have eternal life.

Your Word says we are saved by grace through faith as a gift from You. There is nothing we can do to earn salvation.

I believe and confess with my mouth that Jesus Christ is Your Son. I believe He died on the cross for me and bore all of my sins. I believe in my heart that You raised Jesus from the dead.

I ask you to forgive my sins. I confess Jesus as my Lord and ask that you come live in my heart.

Thank you, Father. I am so grateful! In Jesus' name, amen.

If you prayed this prayer - Congratulations - your new life in Christ has begun Champion!

Stirrup!..the Champions!

I was on my way to Guymon, Oklahoma to have Cowboy Church at the pro-rodeo. It was 2011 and we had plans to go to Australia for the 4th time. With "down under" on my mind, I spoke out loud, "Lord, What does it take to impact a nation?"

I was even more suprised and excited when the Holy Spirit spoke in my spirit, ***"Plant the love that I have for them in their hearts, tell them I'm with them, and I want to work through them. Tell them, they are my Champions in the earth and their deeds will be spoken of through eternity."*** Wow! That Word touched my life, and then I took that Word to Australia.

I spoke at a roping school in Warwick, Queensland, Australia; and everyone began to weep. God's presence was so strong! I believe that Word truly expresses the heart of what this ministry has purposed to do for 40 years. Telling people how real, how personal, and how wonderful our heavenly Father's love is for us.

John 3:16 He's with us, inside us, and He has promised He will never ever leave us or forsake us! Wow! Isaiah 41:10 Hebrews 13:5

Finally, He wants every one of His kids to know that we are His Champions in this earth; to do great things, to do exploits. John 14:12 Isaiah 8:18

All He asks us to do is believe Him, launch forward in obedient faith, and never quit until we Win! It's all for His glory!..for His kingdom!

Now is your time! You are His Champion!

I believe God is "stirring up" His people...His champions. He's stirring up our gifts, our destinies,, and our God-given abilities. Putting your foot in the "stir-up" is the first step to getting in the saddle and beginning the ride of your life. The ride that literally goes into eternity! This ride is the difference between heaven and hell for so many.

God has opened giant doors for this ministry to *"WIN"... souls for the kingdom!* Our mandate is to focus on:

YOUTH: We take teams and give away thousands of *God Wants You To Win!* devotionals to FFA youth in states across the nation, and at the national FFA convention. We also continue to reach out to youth in rodeo all over the world.

PRISONS: Our goal is to continue distributing free devotionals in prisons state by state.

NATIVE AMERICANS: We are returning to the National First Nations Rodeo Finals in Las Vegas. We are advancing toward covering more reservations in North America.

SPANISH: Recently, we printed 20,000 new devotionals in spanish. They have gone all over the USA, Cuba, Mexico, and other hispanic nations. We are now planning our next trip to Cuba. This DOOR is massive!

UKRAINE/RUSSIAN: We went with our "Champ to the Ukraine" Spud Tindell, and have plans to return. So far, we have printed around 100,000 *God Wants You To Win!* devotionals in russian. The response has been phenomenal!

JESUS CHRIST
CHAMPION OF CHAMPIONS

Testimonies

⸘⸘⸘

Mr. Jeff Copenhaver, I don't even know where to begin. I just finished your book "*God Wants You To Win!.*" I've never been moved by anything the way this devotional moved me. I'm 6'6" tall, weigh around 250 lbs., and I'm covered in tattoos and scars. All a testament to the sort of life I've lived. With all honesty, I could barely read this devotional thru a steady flow of tears. Your words, stories, everything about this, especially your love for these magnificent animals that played such an integral role in your everyday life, moved me to tears! It was just an awesome experience. Thank you so much for sharing such an inspirational work of art, literature and divinity all in one. I love it. It helped renew my faith completely. I've asked GOD into my life and prayed the Prayer of Salvation. This time I really and truly said it from my heart though, I meant it. Thank you so much. Keep up the awesome work. I'll be sharing your book with everyone I come into contact with. Anything else that you can spare, I promise to do the same.

Thanks Again, I can't express my gratitude enough.
Sincerely, J.D.W.

⸘⸘⸘

Jeff, Sir, I'd just like you to know that "*God Wants you to Win*" dearly helped me. It helped me focus on Jesus and let me know that He is there for me. Through it all, ups and downs, left and right, Jesus is always there. Your book gave me hope!

Dear Jeff Copenhaver I am 18 years old and I am currently in jail. I asked the security guard if I could go to the library that they have here and he said "sure". I came across your book *"God Wants You to Win."* I can honestly say this is the most powerful book that I have ever read. Truly an amazing book! I've always had a place in my heart for Jesus but before I came to jail I was just a wild teenager who thought he was invincible. I've had two near-death accidents in my life and I have never thanked the Lord that I am still alive on this earth. I never thanked the Lord for anything I had and took everything for granted. I am a freshman in college but I got into some serious trouble last September. I was like a wild chicken with his head cutoff partying literally 24-7. My life was a mess drinking non stop. The judge gave me so many chances and finally got fed up with me and threw me in jail over Christmas break. It's December 25 as I'm writing this and it's around 1:30 in the morning. I just finished the book before writing this. To cut to the chase, your book has literally made my life turn a 180. You Jeff have literally opened my eyes and made me see what lies ahead of me for the good following in the steps of my Lord and savior Jesus Christ. Again thank you so much for opening my eyes and changing my perspective on life and making me a 100 times closer to Jesus. Again the prayer of salvation was a powerful and amazing prayer. Thank you for lifting me up and putting me on my feet again. I am ready to begin my new life in Christ! Your life is not about you anymore, it's about Him living in you! Galatians 2:20 I'm Ready!

Dear Jeff I called you some time ago and you sent me your book *God Wants You to Win!*

I met my husband at a rodeo. He was a bull rider and I was a barrel racer. We've been married now for 12 years. Ive always depended on my husband for love, support and someone I could trust.

This past year we lost our 18 year old son to suicide, and our 21 year old son is in jail on serious charges.

This has been a lot to handle. My spouse has become addicted to crack cocaine and wild women. My life is in shambles. I feel we've reaped from turning away from God. My question is; Is it possible to send your book God wants you to win to my husband?

I personally loved it and I personally feel because of the nature of the book He would take interest in reading it. I'd really like him to have this particular book. This is in hopes God will get hold of his heart, and I can have my spouse back. Thank you Jeff.

My wife Sherry and I cried as we read this letter and prayed that God would turn this situation around. I wrote an entire message on the inside cover of the *God Wants You to Win* devotional that I sent him. Well, get ready! Exactly one month later I received a thank you card. Here's what it said.

My wife wrote you about me, and you sent me your book. I absolutely love the book and I'm now attending church once again. Thanks for your help. Love from Christ's army is amazing!

Jeff, I just wanted you to know that since I last wrote you I have read your book, *God Wants You to Win*, 3 more times and I have seven pages of scripture and just cowboy funny stuff. I can't remember when I've enjoyed a book so much!

Mr. Copenhaver,

I just finished your book "God Wants You To Win!". That was the most inspirational book I've ever read, I'm in Logan County jail, in Guthrie, Oklahoma, I sat and read it aloud to my other three cellies. We're on 23 hour lockdown, so we spend a lot of time reading our bibles as well.

We all prayed the salvation prayer in the back of your book. I don't know about them, but the whole time something kept tugging at my heart the entire time I was reading.

I'm writing to ask you if you could send my wife a copy of your book. My wife and I have been married going on 5 years and we have never had God in our marriage, and I'm crying as I write this, cause I know that is exactly what we are missing in our lives.

I just keep praying that it is not too late for us. I keep praying that the Lord will help my wife. I know my bad decisions have caused everything, but I know that my wife needs the Lord in her life and your book would be great for her too.

I just want to tell you Thank You for this great book and God bless you for the wonderful book you wrote to help open my eyes.

Dear Jeff,

My name is O...S... and I am an inmate on the Hughes unit, serving a life have been lock up 33 years. Guess what! I just finished one of you book. God Want You to Win Vol.II. I have been just little of it at time, I have had this for months, but today I Seg. I pick up this book at cannot put it down! I had read the Whole book now. Before I finishes it I fine myself given my life to Jesus Christ!

I had given up all my wrong doing. I have gave up the things that I live on to make money. I throw away, it was hard cause I had this evil spirit telling me to hold to it, tail get out and sell them. for awhile I did hold to it! But the Lord told me to get ridly of it.

I listen to Jesus this day Sunday and gave up to Him, now I am a new man in Jesus. I will not go on my feelings I will go on my faith! If you can, I would like to receive some of your books. Can you send me Dios Quiere Que Ganes! or God Wants You To Win! I would like to have them both!

Thank You,   O. S.

God is Good, My God be with you! Smile.

Dear Jeff, I want to thank you so much for writing, *God Wants You to Win!* My son is in prison for the second time for drugs. He has only been there for about two months. He said they assigned him to bunk 19 and he found your volume 2 there and read it. He said page 19 and 20 opened his eyes, since then he has been saved and is going to be baptized as soon as he can. I know God left that book for him. Thank you God bless.

Some friends of ours were pulling onto the highway in front of their house when they spy something a little different. A hitchhiker was standing on the side of the road with a saddle next to him.

Ordinarily the dad wouldn't pick up a hitchhiker with his family aboard but this time he made an exception. The man with the saddle seemed friendly and visibly hungry so they invited him to their house for lunch. As they were eating, the hitchhiker said, "I have two earthly possessions. One is the saddle you saw me with, the other is this book." That's when he pulled out his, *God Wants You to Win*, devotional. This book has touched my life! Can I read you one of the stories? He began to read them a story. This book had changed his life! One of his two earthly possessions!

It had been a rough year for Randy -- really rough! Financial difficulties were more than a Sheriff's salary could deal with He was losing his place and in the midst of this his wife found someone else and left with their children. After considering his options he finally decided there was no hope for him; nothing to live for. With a pistol in his hand moments from eternity he noticed a book on his kitchen table that he had received at a horse sale. The title caught his attention, *"God Wants You to Win."* He began to read it and read some more. Today this man is on fire for the Lord!

———— ∞∞∞ ————

My friend Dave Burrows and his family have passed out thousands of *"God Wants You to Win"* devotionals. One year he went to a huge dance and barbecue in the Texas panhandle to give away several hundred devotionals. This was basically one loud, wild party. Dave isn't bashful so in the midst of the music he puts books on the stage for the band then starts walking at the bottom of the grandstands giving more books away. Then he said people in the stands began to wave at him to get his attention. They were wanting books by the hundreds. At one point he said the music was cranked up to deafening and the song was, "I like my women a little on the trashy side." I share that to paint the setting for you. Right then Dave said a lady with short shorts and a bikini top walked up to him and asked him if she could have a book. He gave her one. She had a beer in one hand and a devotional in another! The thought hit him that life had treated her rough. Dave said the moment he gave her the book he felt the presence of God so strong! His love and mercy! Dave was thankful to have a tool like, *God Wants You to Win*, that the people were interested in and that would change their lives!

———— ∞∞∞ ————

Our friends David and Pat Young live in Canadian, Tx. They have literally given away thousands of devotionals in every imaginable place and situation. One day David gave a *God Wants You to Win* devotional to a Spanish speaking lady at a grocery store in Canadian. A few months after that I was speaking at David's church and that lady walked up to me and told me her story. She took the book home and read it but she already knew the Lord. She then gave it to her husband and he loved it and got saved praying the prayer at the end. Then he gave it to his son and God touched the son through the book. Now get this...before all this, the wife said the father and son would get together every week to drink because they were both alcoholics. She said they still get together every week only now their reason is to read the *God Wants You to Win* book together! She was ecstatic to say the least! The Latino culture loves this book!

<hr />

As we headed to the Championship Roughstock Challenge, being held New Years Eve, my son (who has just turned 12) was tied for first place in the Jr. Bull Division. He was defending his title, as last year he was Champion. At the end of the day, he did not cover and ended up being second....which in this particular year end challenge.... held no accolades. He congratulated the winners and turned to get his gear. I saw him hide his face, to hide the tears streaming down his cheeks. I could not hold back my tears.... Our family of 5 loaded up to head back to our home town. Each of us telling him how proud we were of him. Winning is not what makes us proud. His relationship with the Lord, his family, his friends.... his character is what brings us pride. He told us he knew he should not be sad, as he knew it was his performance that cost him the title. He never spoke poorly of any other contestants. During the event various vendors were selling different items, a very kind vendor had handed us a CD and each of us a complimentary book.... messages from Jeff Copenhaver. After a few miles I decided to pop the CD in,,,, looking to help get our minds off of the broken hearted feeling that my son was carrying. We knew immediately, God had a plan with the messages. We listened the entire ride home...feeling encouraged and touched by the words....words from a man who speaks the Word of God. The stories and lessons were so applicable to what we were experiencing. I saw my son's eyes as they began to show light instead of sorrow....He began to speak of next season, and how he'll learn from this. He began to chuckle at parts of the stories. I would like to thank Jeff Copenhaver and the gentleman who was handing out the CD's.... I am so sorry to say I did not get his name... These men will never know how much of a gift these messages were at the exact moment they were needed. We are a strong Christian family and were able to receive strength from these words at a time that we were all feeling down.

Thank you for your words, for your messages, for following the Lord....

Thank you from this mom and her son....from all of us.

...and God Wants YOU to Win as well!
GO FOR IT!

Jeff signing books at FFA youth convention.

Dear Jeff and Sherry,

My leap of faith. My son brought your book back from the National FFA Convention. I read it. The book was a blessing when I needed it. I'm unemployed, haven't found employment yet. Total income for October was $310. So here's my 1/10th. I don't belong to a church but I need some place to send my tithes to.

I will let you know how things go. This is the first time I've ever tithed, so I am going to just do it.

The book was really good. I am hoping the rest of the family reads it. I started reading the bible about 6 months ago and something that I've learned is faith is a process.
I am just going for it. - Sandra

"God Wants You To Win!" books

     In 2005 I compiled several of the monthly articles that I was writing for *Western World publications* and put them together as a book. I titled it, *"God Wants You To Win!"*

     We printed thousands of volume 1, and in 2012 I finished volume 2. Recently in 2017, I finished a 3 in 1 book; the best of volume 1 and volume 2, plus a new volume 3 called, **God Wants You To Win!**

     This book is about real-life stories. People love these books, from the "cowboy" covers to the dynamic stories inside. We have been overwhelmed and excited by the life changing testimonies we receive daily. As of 2018, we have printed and given away "free" OVER HALF A MILLION BOOKS! They also have been translated into spanish and russian.

     In december of 2017, we handed out over 10,000 free books at Mandalay Bay and Sands Convention Center in Las Vegas during the **National Finals Rodeo**.

In 2018, we gave out thousands of books to the **FFA youth** at various conventions, including their National Convention.

     I would like to personally thank everyone who has helped, prayed for, and supported this ministry. For the many lives that have been dramatically changed; your help, your generosity, has made it all possible.

     One time, I was praying for needs we were facing in the ministry. Very softly, the Lord spoke in my heart, "I will provide through my Champions!"

     Thank you for being a partner...a Champion... to this ministry!

                         -Jeff Copenhaver

Every year at the **NFR**, as I look around the crowd, I see hope for America in a cowboy setting. A remnant of godly people that remain attached to the principles that make our nation great. Your involvement will help us to continue and expand this work.

GOING TO THE RODEO WORLD, WESTERN WORLD, AND THE WORLD

GOD WANTS YOU TO Win!

WITH THE LOVE OF JESUS CHRIST.

JEFF COPENHAVER MINISTRIES

Jeff Copenhaver Ministries
P.O. Box 37
Rainbow, Texas 76077

www.jeffcopenhaver.com

Over half a million devotionals
given away free worldwide!
...in english, spanish, and russian.

Notes